How To Win With

Information

Or Lose Without It

By Andrew P. Garvin
and Hubert Bermont

Published by
BERMONT BOOKS

twenty-six dollars

ISBN 0-930686-08-X

OUR NEW
ADDRESS
P. O. Box 309
Glenelg, Md. 21737
(301) 531-3560

Printed in the United States of America

Contents

Acknowledgements

I wish to express my sincere thanks to all the dedicated, professional people who have worked for and with me in the information business throughout the past ten years. Without them, this book would not have been possible. In particular, special contributions were made by Kathleen Bingham, Neal McIlvaine, Elke Kastner, Anne Potter and Tom Miller.

I also want to thank my friend Geri Carranza, who unknowingly provided the inspiration needed to complete this book.

Andrew P. Garvin

Foreword

When Andy Garvin first told me that he wanted to write a book about raising our information consciousness in our new information environment, I became immediately enthusiastic. As a bookman for twenty-four years, I knew that such a book by someone with his talent and vast store of knowledge would be of immense value. When later he asked if I would co-author this book, I had ambivalent feelings: pride that he had selected me, and fear of my own inadequacy as a "team player."

Fortunately, we worked well and smoothly together. Hopefully the reader will find this book as much of a learning experience as I did while helping to create it.

Hubert Bermont

Introduction

The most important thing for business and professional people to have is the most difficult thing for them to find. Information. Information makes the difference between a decision and a guess, between success and failure, between wealth and poverty.

Knowledge is power. The amount of power required to be successful and to influence people and decisions depends directly upon the amount of knowledge you have. Knowledge results from information. And how to become the kind of individual who can acquire valuable information quickly, easily and economically is the subject of this book.

Speaking of books, it is worth noting ruefully that they are published in spates. When a subject is "hot," a number of publishers jump into the fray with pertinent titles; but mostly the books pretty much say the same thing. The subject of information is indeed the hottest. However, we have no intention of repeating what the others are saying. There are many fine *source* books available that will tell you all about hundreds and hundreds of valuable sources of information, many of which you can probably use. Among the most notable of these is Lorna Daniells' *Business Information Sources* (University of California Press, 1976). This is no such sourcebook— despite the helpful appendices.

There are also many how-to books that explain, usually in technical terms, how to perform market research. They will tell you about the different kinds of research, about designing surveys and performing tabulations and about a great variety of techniques that the average executive doesn't want to be bothered with. Among the best of these is the *Handbook Of Marketing Research*, edited by Robert Ferber (McGraw-Hill, 1974). Interestingly, Mr. Ferber has even put together a sourcebook on how-to books in the field called *A Basic Bibliography On Market Research* (American Marketing Association, 1974). Our book is not a how-to book, although we'll try to tell you something about how to be an effective information gatherer.

This book is unique in that it is the first (and, as yet, only) one to deal specifically with raising your *information consciousness.*

Until this consciousness is enhanced, all the sourcebooks and how-to books in the world will be of little value to you, because there will be no impetus to go to them. This is in the same way that a student needs reading readiness to learn to read. *Information consciousness* is the key—and raising yours is the purpose of this book.

Raising your information consciousness means learning how to think in ways that result in your being well informed, in being infinitely more *resourceful* than you are now. This is not easy, but it is far more accessible than solving problems in nuclear physics.

To be well informed takes time, effort, curiosity and some thought. You have to be able to ask the right questions and to understand how the right answers may be found. If you can find the right information, you can use it to gain knowledge. Clearly, the more you know about something, the better you can deal with it, the more you can *control* your own situation. Knowledge is a synthesis of information. And knowing means winning.

It is curious to see how many people have no idea how to find what they need to know. It is *astonishing* to see how many executives and professionals don't even realize when they need information, whether or not it can be obtained, or, if so, how valuable it can be to them.

The evidence is everywhere. Ask a group of executives if they can briefly explain the information contained in such basic information sources as the *Statistical Abstract Of The United States,* or *Thomas' Register,* or the *Business Periodicals Index,* or the *F&S Index Of Corporations & Industries,* or the *Congressional Quarterly.* We'll wager no one in the group can correctly answer. (Don't worry if you can't either. The purpose of this book is to raise your consciousness so you'll *want to be able to answer.*)

More evidence: A study published in the *Harvard Business Review* revealed that only about 8% of the businesses represented by 1,200 survey participants had a department with trained employees to gather and analyze information about competitors. In smaller firms, the percentage was considerably lower. Consider this for a moment. To survive in business—indeed in life—you must constantly compete. Everyone knows this. Yet over 90% of the businesses in this survey had no formal program to gather information about their competition!

The collective suffering caused by inadequate information gathering is, of course, immeasurable. But it is evident everywhere in professional, business and even personal failures.

Many of the failures are big and complex. The Edsel is a classic example. But others can be perceived in everyone's day-to-day activities. Think back on your own experiences and those of people you know. How many times have you been a loser because you didn't have a key piece of information in advance? You overpaid for goods and services because you didn't know they were available cheaper elsewhere. You wasted hours standing in the wrong line. You vainly tried to obtain something from a government bureaucracy armed with the wrong papers. You went on vacation and ended up in a dismal, miserable place.

We all know about and have been exposed to Intelligence Quotients all of our lives. But what is your individual *Information Quotient?* There is, of course, no such thing as yet, because no one has developed one. Perhaps someday *we* will. We would undoubtedly find that people with a high level of information consciousness have the following characteristics:

— They tend to read a lot.
— They keep lots of files on all kinds of things.
— They have an insatiable curiosity.
— They prefer an authoritative opinion to gossip.

In short, these people enjoy a high degree of information literacy.

Recently, we were at a popular seaside resort where a few local motels competed for the tourist business. In booking a room in one of the motels, we by chance discovered that the owner had absolutely no idea what rates were being charged by his competitor located less than half a mile away! It was not surprising to learn some months later that the owner's motel had been taken over by a small hotel chain. He had lost his business.

This book was not written solely for the executive in a big corporation. It is written for all executives everywhere, and for professionals, scientists, consultants, technicians, and, yes, even motel owners. While our emphasis will be on business and professions, the lessons of this book apply to all of life, for if you cannot use information to create business successes, then it is doubtful you can use information for personal achievement either.

In "The Paper Chase," which deals with the rigors and vicissitudes of law school, the professor addresses the neophytes with this combined warning and promise: You come in here with a head full of mush, and when you finish—if you succeed—you will leave thinking like a lawyer.

To paraphrase: You open this book with a head full of false assumptions, but when you close it—if you have paid attention—you will think like an information genius.

CHAPTER 1

Information: Keystone of the Future

Why, you might well ask, is it so important to raise my information consciousness?

Perhaps failures resulting from lack of information seem remote to you. Perhaps you are successful already. You don't seem to need much information. It may be that the most important reason to elevate your awareness of the world of information is not to avoid present failures, but to maximize future opportunities and minimize future problems.

The future, in fact, promises to bring an environment in which the people who know how to acquire, store, access, distribute and control information stand to have more power than they have ever had before in the history of mankind.

That's a sweeping statement, but we make it with full confidence. The decades ahead are going to bring profound information-related changes to our society. Those who are not prepared for them will be left behind.

Let's take a quick look at some of the changes that will create a need for a higher information consciousness.

The increasing complexity of the world is already churning up demand for more information. When societies are confronted with fast-moving political and economic crises, with energy shortages, with environmental protection problems and more complicated regulations, the ability to deal with these is directly related to increased understanding, which in turn, is based on information.

With forecasts of double-digit inflation, high interest rates and increased government intervention, the business community is trying to find new ways to deal with an atmosphere potentially hostile to profitable growth. People are talking about trying shorter product-development cycles, better returns on new products, higher fixed-asset utilization, maximization of revenues from existing customers, less expensive marketing and physical distribution channels, tighter cash management, more efficient compliance. These types of resourceful strategies all create an enormous demand for the acquisition and management of information.

Demographic changes will also profoundly affect our future. Between 1980 and 1990 alone, extraordinary changes will take place in the U.S. population. The ranks of the high-income, free-spending, middle-aged 35 to 44-year-olds will swell by an astounding 50%, as compared to an overall population gain of 11%. The "graying of America" will accelerate with the 65-and-older age group increasing by 24%. Meanwhile, the population of teens and young adults will decline dramatically. Consider what information demands these changes will create: we'll need data on new products, new markets, changing attitudes and values of older people; we'll need better understanding of the decline in youth culture values; we'll need, in fact, information on a whole new America. On a more personal level, consider that 35 to 44-year-olds are the prime source of middle managers. With their numbers increasing, there may be too many people for too few jobs. Performance—and the information to maximize it—will be at a premium.

Information will also be necessary to improve the stagnating productivity level of the American worker. U.S. productivity growth is now the lowest of all the major industrial nations. Since 1950, for example, Japan's annual productivity growth rate has been *four times* that of the U.S. Business leaders are calling for a halt to the declining trend in productivity. More efficient information management can make it happen.

As changes create a need for more information, the *value* of information will begin to increase significantly. Already experts are predicting an "information society."

The Diebold Group, a leading management consulting and forecasting firm, sees a basic shift in job orientation from people to information. Advances in technology, communications and computers—wedded with a bigger appetite for information—will give managers access to a plethora of computerized information files on their industries, competitors, suppliers and customers as well as on nationwide and worldwide economic data. With so much information around, corporations will be organized around information rather than work flow.

To quote John Diebold, Chairman of The Diebold Group: "Information will be recognized as a valuable resource on the same level as capital and labor. We shall abandon this long period when—perhaps because of its abundance in a period of growing scarcity—information has been consistently underpriced and underutilized, and its contribution underrated."

(*Newsweek*, Sept. 17, 1979, Special Section, "Decision Making in the 1980's")

Actually, a new information environment is already here and is actively being used by sophisticated executives (see chapter 6). Some are even talking about the emergence of an "information economy" in both the private and public sectors. An information economy is one that is based on the flow of information, i.e. information in one form or another comprises the major part of the gross national product. Information industry leaders have opened new areas of products and services, ranging from reference books to computers. New conferences such as the National Information Conference and Exposition are fostering the development of a community of users as well as the emerging profession of information management. Even the White House has a new information center.

The message of the future is clear. The successful executives and professionals will be those who have mastered the art of being information conscious.

CHAPTER 2

Information Versus Assumption

Wial, exactly, is information? Dictionary definitions equate it with knowledge. But knowledge is the *result* of information. Information consists of facts, news, statistics, impressions—pieces of *intelligence* that singly or together increase your awareness.

What is an assumption? It is a conclusion based upon none of the above. It is the spanning of a non-existent synapse. It is a conclusion sometimes luckily true, but most often false, which is derived from nothing at all. It springs full-blown without any evidence. It is birthed by an attitude which says, "I *should* know this, so I *do.*" In short, it comes from an oversized ego. A case in point:

A book publisher (name withheld for reasons of embarrassment) recently decided to publish an annual anthology of in-depth articles concerning a profession with which he was very familiar. He reckoned that he needed only thirty such meaningful pieces to make a fine book. Since there were *probably* one hundred and fifty such articles published in any given year, it would be simple to acquire them, winnow the best, and write for permission to reprint. He retained a "clipping service" to find them at a high monthly fee. After three months (and several hundred dollars), he was dismayed to find—nothing. He had made the *assumption* that such articles existed, because he thought they *should*. Had he gone to an information retrieval service, he would have learned this in ten minutes at a small fraction of the cost (more about this later). But to have done the latter, it would have been necessary to side-step his enormous ego and *ask a question* rather than *assume a fact*.

Another common wrong assumption based upon a malfunctioning ego is, "I am the only one who has ever thought of this problem (question)." Not true. Ninety-nine chances out of a hundred many others have asked the same question. And probably they have come up with the answer or the solution. Furthermore, that answer is usually available to you!

Information professionals are constantly amazed at the false assumptions which fill their clients' heads. People who seek information usually think that certain data are easy to find when difficult, difficult to find when easy, cheap to buy when expensive, expensive when cheap, etc. All are assumptions with no basis in fact.

Information is obtained only by asking questions. Here is an approach to a problem made by an executive who had previously succeeded in raising his level of information consciousness:

A New York firm considered placing a permanent representative in Chicago. Never having had this experience before, the head of the firm wondered how he could interact with this representative in the most productive manner. His first realization was that other companies must have had the same problem at one time or another. He ordered a search for literature on the subject of sales representation outside of home territory. He discovered a marvelous article telling him everything he wanted to know.

It makes no difference whether you are the head of a company seeking a new plant site, a marketing executive looking for new sales opportunities, a dentist opening a new office, a grocer moving into a new neighborhood, or a consultant seeking new clients and/or new opportunities for your old clients—you need information. That information is usually available, at a price. That information, properly interpreted, leads to success.

Your assumptions will lead to failure.

Herein lies perhaps the most fundamental concept in information consciousness. At the risk of boring you, we'll repeat it: Rather than making any assumptions that might lead to failure, make the assumption that the information needed for success is out there somewhere and available at a reasonable price. Then go look for it.

The reason that the information you need is probably out there at a reasonable price is that someone, somehow, somewhere had a problem similar to yours and may already have collected, stored and published the information in some form. And today, it is infinitely easier to find that information than it was fifty, twenty or even ten years ago. If it is easier to find, it is also likely to be cheaper to find. This is the benefit that lies at the core of the information world we are in.

One word of caution, though. Just because the information you need is *likely* to be available at a reasonable price, doesn't mean it *will* be. Don't assume a certainty. Common sense should prevail. For example, it is clearly probable that statistics on consumption of soft drinks in the U.S. are available, but it is obviously a lot more unlikely that anyone has already collected figures on how many residents of Park Avenue in New York's Manhattan drink Gatorade.

Another reason that people are prone to making assumptions (aside from their egotistical near-sightedness) is that there is no education on the subject of accurate information-gathering. This is somewhat akin to the wild assumptions most of us made about sex before formal sex education came to the schools. At best, there are only a handful of courses specifically devoted to information. The typical pattern has always been: you had to write a paper, so you went to the library to do "research," this consisted of going through the card-catalogue file to find something of interest, finding those books and periodicals, and finally writing the paper. Today you are in the business or professional world. That method usually has no relevance to what you are doing, because you are not writing a paper. You are attempting to survive in a highly competitive world!

Actually, some professionals are much better trained in understanding the vital importance of research skills. Lawyers, for example, rely heavily on casebooks. Doctors must continuously consult reference books to be up-to-date on drugs. But in general, management information requirements are rarely as precise. This, combined with managers' diverse education and former emphasis on "research-for-papers," produces executives who are woefully unprepared to use information for current business needs and decisions.

When we speak of information consciousness, we are in many ways speaking about a level of understanding concerning the degree to which information is involved with decision-making. Making decisions is, after all, what executives are supposed to do. So if you are going to make effective decisions, you must be fully aware that they are the outcome of a process that involves measurement, fact-gathering, interpretation, analysis and forecasting.

In extremely simplified terms, to make a decision, you've got to do your homework. It's amazing how many people fail to appreciate this fully and proceed to make their decisions with little or no information, or preparation.

To use an example from personal life, how many times have friends of yours complained that they went off on vacation only to be faced with transportation problems, over-booked hotels, wasted time, bad weather, poor food and service? This type of thing rarely happens to people who are information conscious. When they decide to go somewhere, they do their homework. They have maps, they know weather statistics, they are armed with hotel and restaurant ratings; they've studied articles on the resort. They enjoy their vacation.

Some people say that being too prepared creates a lack of adventure; there are no surprises. This may be true in your personal life (though how many *good* surprises can you think of), but in business, you can't afford any surprises.

One of the first steps toward improving the use of information is the achievement of a clear understanding of the different forms of information.

At the beginning of this chapter, we defined information as pieces of intelligence that singly or together increase your awareness. Knowledge, we said, is the result of information.

Similarly, information can be said to be the result of data. Data consist of raw numbers and facts. Information consists of *meaningful* numbers and facts. Information involves the addition of a certain *value* to data through some level of selection, interpretation or re-arrangement.

If you want to know the chance of rain in Chicago in May, and you obtain reams of weather statistics for the city for the past hundred years, all you have is data. But if you have, on a single page, a set of statistics that shows, for each of the past hundred years, the percentage of days of rain in May, with an average at the bottom, then you have information. You have knowledge on which to base a decision or take action.

Another important distinction to make is between *primary* information and *secondary* information. Awareness of the difference between the two can prevent serious mistakes.

Primary information is that which is originated and developed directly from a source, usually in response to a specific need. It may loosely be defined as first-hand information. Secondary information is just what its name implies—it's second-hand. It is information which is already in existence, having been collected at some prior point in time by other people; and it may have been changed and reinterpreted somehow when put to second use.

If you perform a survey of people's preferences for different brands of cereal, the results of the survey will be primary information to you. If you then write an article for a magazine on the cereal consumption of consumers, and if you incorporate a summary of the results of your survey, then the information in the article will be secondary information to the magazine's readers.

The distinction may seem obvious here, but an understanding of the distinction is a key to the use of information in business situations. One reason is that primary information is usually expensive to gather, while secondary information—having been already collected by someone else—is usually inexpensive. If you were interested in consumer preferences of cereals, it would cost you several thousand dollars to commission a survey, but only a fraction of that to obtain the information already published in a magazine. The trick, of course, is to find out about the existence of that magazine article. And the problem, as well as the opportunity, with secondary information is that there is an enormous amount of it available.

Another key distinction is the difference between *internal* and *external* information. In a business context, internal information involves facts about your own company. Your sales figures, the number of clients you have, where your products are shipped, etc. Internal information is used mostly—though not exclusively—for the purpose of measuring performance. External information, on the other hand, is information about the world outside your company. It involves facts about your competitors, about markets, demographics, the environment, etc. External information is used mostly for planning and decision-making, although it is obvious that an effective decision to move into a new market, for example, should be based on a careful assessment of internal information (what markets are we in now) and external information (where are the opportunities). Obvious, that is, to anyone except the vast majority of executives who every day make key decisions either without much external information at all, or without bothering to combine the external with the internal.

It should be added that internal information is usually readily available to most of us, because it is necessary and vital to be collected in order for a business to operate. When Xerox and IBM talk about information, they are actually referring to internal information because that's the kind of information their equipment is most useful in managing. It's also the kind of information most businesses *must* have organized. External information is not usually perceived as being that important, is more difficult to obtain, and is often neglected—with occasionally disastrous consequences.

The business press is replete with stories of companies and products that failed because changes in the marketplace or demographics—external information—were ignored or never perceived.

Those who inaccurately assume that their assumptions are correct may accurately assume that they will fall by the wayside.

CHAPTER 3

What is the Question?

It is told that when the great Gertrude Stein was on her deathbed, a friend came to visit and found Ms Stein in her final throes. Thrashing around on her hospital bed, somewhat delerious, she kept repeating over and over, "What is the answer? What is the answer?" Hoping to hear a final philosophic pronunciamento, the friend leaned forward expectantly. As she expired, Gertrude Stein's final words were, "But then—what is the question?" Probably apocryphal, but the tale attests to the heightened information consciousness of that wonderful lady of letters.

What *is* your question? Do you know? Ofttimes the question you ask is either obtuse or not the question you really mean to ask. Moreover, it is usually asked in the wrong way. An ancient Greek philosopher once said that a problem without a solution is usually a problem which is put the wrong way. Similarly, a question which is unanswerable is usually a question which is put the wrong way. Incorrect questions are the single greatest cause of information failures.

Computers nowadays contain enormous amounts of retrievable information. If you were to ask of a computer, for example, "How can I best sell corn flakes in Brazil?" you would get no meaningful answer. As a matter of fact, computers usually cannot answer "how" questions at all. But if you were to ask a computer for information on "Brazil" and "corn flakes," you would get all the information you need on that subject to draw intelligent conclusions, which, in turn, would be the answer to your original question.

You may say, "Well, it seems as though I must know what I am looking for beforehand in order to find it." Sometimes you *can* know this. Sometimes you can't. But if you have raised your information consciousness, you will at least know the *procedures* to follow—the thinking process—that will assist you in finding out what you are looking for.

If you don't have questions about your profession or your business or the ways in which you are conducting them—*you should question that!* It means you have a very low level of information consciousness. And you are not alone. When asked what is the single biggest sales resistance they encounter, the salesmen of a leading information and research service firm reported very simply that business executives say they have no questions!

What is lacking at this low level of consciousness?

Interestingly, most executives will readily admit they have plenty of *problems.* So the first thing lacking is the ability to think of problems (and opportunities) as information needs, as series of questions that need to be answered. EVERY PROBLEM THAT RELATES TO A BUSINESS OR PROFESSION ULTIMATELY BOILS DOWN TO AN INFORMATION PROBLEM. We think we have decision problems. But if we had a sufficient amount of information, all correct decisions would be inherent in that information. That's why it's so important, when thinking about problems, to think information. That's information consciousness.

Another reason for a low level of information consciousness is the lack of the *discipline* of a logical progression of thought. Let us assume that you want to eat at a very fine French restaurant next Saturday evening. Lack of this discipline would find you downtown that evening without a reservation, poking your head into a number of restaurants, checking prices and menus, being turned away by some, etc. In short, a hassle. The proper reaction to this problem by a person with a high level of information consciousness would be: "My problem is to find a good French restaurant. So I need information about restaurants. Someone has probably had the same problem before, so there must be something written on this subject. It is probably a guidebook on restaurants in this area. It may indicate which are French, plus other facts on prices, hours, atmosphere. So if I find the guidebook, I solve my problem." Obviously, this is a simplified example. But the principle can be applied universally. It bespeaks a mind disciplined to think in terms of information steps.

A young lady we know had a very typical problem. She spent three years in a liberal arts college, then spent ten years in Italy married to an actor. While there she became fluent in Italian and did some odd jobs translating, dubbing films, etc. She later obtained a divorce and returned to New York, desperately needing a job. She had no college degree, no office skills and had never held a real full-time job. For days she floundered around visiting friends of friends who supposedly would help her and contacting employment agency after agency where all she was asked was how many words a minute she could type. Finally she consulted us. We applied some information discipline. The problem was to find a job. The lady's assets included intelligence, language, affinity for the film business and other creative arts, and a background from Italy. The information steps required were:

— Get a list of all Italian companies with offices in New York.

— Contact all of them with priority on those involved in the arts.

— Visit the commercial attaché of the Italian consulate to find out what companies might be expanding or opening offices in New York.

— Find out which employment agencies specialize in bilingual jobs and which specialize in the music and film industry. Restrict visits to those.

— Get a list of all companies in New York in the film, recording, artistic management, music and television industries. Contact them.

— Also get a list of all leading translation firms.

The young lady found an excellent position.

The embarrassment of not knowing what you think you should know can also lead to a low level of information consciousness. This is exemplified by the millions of people who absolutely refuse to ask for directions from a police officer or gas station attendant. They prefer to "find it themselves." They usually get lost. Getting lost is losing. Getting there is winning.

Let's face it: "know-it-alls" know nothing; they are always making assumptions.

Okay, you have now attained the discipline of thinking in information terms. So when you need information, you ask someone a question. When you get an answer, you find that it's not the answer to the question you thought you asked. Examine your question again. Many talented technicians, businessmen, consultants and other professionals never learned to ask for information in a way that produces the correct response. Yet you can vastly improve your ability to find and use information. The next time you need information, before you ask anything, first ask yourself these questions:

Why do I need the information?

The reason behind any request is usually obvious, yet a very clear and precise understanding of why information is needed is often lacking. The result is a vague or inappropriate question. For example, if you need a specific fact, like total 1978 sales of Perrier, to toss into a speech, you should ask for exactly that. (A good estimate is readily available.) Asking for a "run-down" on Perrier will surely increase the cost of the research and may not even yield the sales figure. On the other hand, if you need background to help assess the market for a new kind of bottled water, then asking for a profile of the bottled water industry may be an excellent broad question. In any case, tell whoever is going to look for the answer *why* you need it. An understanding of the reason is vital to a successful search.

How do I translate my information need into a question?

Even when you've clearly established why you need information, formulating a good question can be a challenge. For example, assume you believe a sales compensation plan needs revamping. You want information to help you do it. You could ask for any available information on sales compensation plans. Such a request could produce huge masses of mostly useless data. Try asking, "Are there comparative studies of sales compensation plans that will tell me the norms for my industry?" This type of precise question could produce an equally precise answer. (In this case, it's the "Sales Personnel Report from the Executive Compensation Service of the American Management Associations.")

Can I transpose my question to specifics?

Your real question may be a general one. "Will a branch office I am contemplating in Des Moines succeed?" No one can answer this question as stated. But consider some highly specific questions on the subject: What is the population of Des Moines? What are the demographics of that population? What is the political climate of Des Moines? Who are my competitors in Des Moines? Combined, answers to these questions, properly interpreted, will assist you in making an intelligent (successful) decision.

What is the value of the answer to me?

A sense of the value of the answer you expect can help you phrase your question. Do you need the information for a low-priority idea on which you're working? Did the Chairman of the Board ask for it? Is it related to a $10 million new product development plan? If you have some idea of the value of the answer to you, you'll be better able to phrase your question and give critical guidance to a researcher. (You wouldn't want your secretary to spend a full day trying to find a hotel room in New York if there's only a 10% chance you'll go there.) (More on value in Chapter 4).

What do I already know about the answer?

You may already know some information that will help answer your question. For example, you want to know total U.S. distilled spirits sales in dollars, but you already have it in units. Or maybe you know some key sources for the answer you're seeking and you've tried them without success. By all means, tell whoever will do the research about the background information you have and where you've already looked. Much time is lost because people so often neglect to do this.

How available is the information I need?

If you're not a researcher you won't know what data is available and what isn't. But a little careful thought on your part can tell you how likely it is than an answer will be found. For example, common sense suggests that finding a market-share breakdown of baby carriage sales for three counties in Idaho is a virtually impossible task. (It probably can be done only through an extensive, expensive survey.) Asking for a list of all major department and discount stores in the top 40 cities is a question that can probably be answered, but common sense should suggest that it can't be done in fifteen minutes.

Am I prepared to ask the question myself?

Remember the telephone game? Ten people line up, and the first says a brief sentence to the second, who repeats it to the third, and so on. By the time the tenth person has heard the sentence, it has completely changed from what the first person said. If you have a question and want to ask someone to get an answer, don't relay your request through a third party, like your secretary. It will almost insure that the answer you get will not be the one you thought you needed. Always ask your own questions.

Do I need an answer, or just the source?

This is an important distinction most people fail to make, especially when they are using someone else to perform the actual research. Generally, the more specific your question, the more you need the actual answer. If your question is very broad, you may, in fact, wish to browse through the source itself. In the example we used before, concerning your branch office in Des Moines, you might well need answers to the specific questions on population. But, if there were a good factbook on the Des Moines area, you would want to examine it.

Many people in business have told us that even when they are in a frame of mind to ask questions, they're not exactly sure *what to ask questions about.* The reason usually is a feeling that their particular problem or question doesn't relate to any information that may be available.

While we can't tell you what your own questions should be, we can dispel once and for all the notion that information may not be available. YOU CAN AND SHOULD ASK QUESTIONS ABOUT ANYTHING. In most cases information *is* available.

To suggest the endless possibilities, here's a sampling of how key executives in various functions are getting results through answers to questions:

When the president of a major chemical company felt that he might have to justify his R&D expenditures at the next stockholders' meeting, he asked for and got data on the R&D expenditures of ten similar firms.

When back-up data was needed for the development of an electronics company's five-year plan, the planning director obtained information on typical industry financial ratios, articles on current management practices in the electronics business, data on exports, and a study of the industry's future in Europe.

When the chairman of a major chemical company decided to look into potential acquisitions in the solar energy field, he began by obtaining an overview report on the industry which identified three potential targets, two of which were later researched in depth.

A consultant, faced with the problem of helping a client grow in Europe, asked for lists of major projected growth industries in the 80's. He then got the names of leading European firms in those industries.

The marketing director of a company with a new bottled water subsidiary wanted to expand in Florida. He asked for a list of competitors in that state and then commissioned an in-depth study of the industry in Florida, including interviews with companies in the field.

A sales manager scheduled an important meeting with a key prospect. To do his "homework" beforehand, he dug for and unearthed vital facts on the prospective client, biographical details on the principals involved and several published articles on the company and its industry.

A disposable diaper firm became concerned about long range sales forecasts. It collected birth-rate projection statistics through the year 2000 and used them to develop year-by-year data on the size of its potential market.

A printing products manufacturer wanted to introduce a new line. He obtained an overview of the market, had an outside company research the alternative methods of distribution to end users and commissioned a survey of distributors. He was then able to competently determine his product introduction strategy.

Faced with foreign currency exchange-rate problems, the financial officer of a medium-sized firm decided to ask for a list of companies that are in the business of projecting exchange rates. He got his list and used one of the companies to help him significantly reduce his losses.

A large company was interested in how contact lens accessories could be better sold through drug store chains. They commissioned a survey of the managers of the optical centers in major drug chain outlets.

A public relations manager who needed to develop a campaign concerning diabetes figured that celebrities could help. He asked for and got a list of famous people who have the disease.

A company president's son was seriously ill with a form of colitis. Instead of merely consulting the leading local specialist, the president first obtained a list of virtually every article on the disease published in medical journals over the past ten years. Then he obtained copies of the articles, read them, and through them identified the four or five leading specialists on the disease in the world. He also obtained background on the major drugs used to treat the disease. Then, he took his son to the best doctors, armed with sufficient knowledge to discuss the case intelligently with those doctors.

And here is a typical and actual list of information needs recently handled for business executives and consultants by a qualified information retrieval service:

How many new ammonia plants have been built since 1975 in the U.S.? Also give location.

What was last year's consumption of imported beer? How much was imported from each country?

Consumption trend of tequila? Rate of growth; percent of population or households drinking? Is it seasonal?

How many wearers of contact lenses are there in the U.S.A.? Are there any breakouts by male/female and by age?

What was the brand name, manufacturer and year of introduction of the first electric telegraph machine? Office typewriter? Copying machine?

Obtain a list of the celebrities who have appeared in the Teacher's Scotch ad campaign?

What is the profitability of the health club business?

Are there any businesses with U.S. offices that specialize in the rental of ski chalets and apartments in Europe?

Number of patients on hemodialysis, with breakdown for patients newly placed on dialysis annually. Also, what percentage of dialysis patients have hypertension?

Please put together a list of experts in potato chips.

Do a computer search for information on "no" and "low" cholesterol products as replacements for ice cream, butter, milk and eggs. What is the market size now for each of those replacement items?

Provide a bibliography on dimethylglycine.

Obtain some books of cartoons done by past American political cartoonists whose works are now in the public domain.

What is the cat population of the U.S.? How many live in the metropolitan areas?

What were the top two songs for 1923, 1933, 1945, 1950, 1967?

Bibliography of recent books or articles on aphrodisiacs and hangover cures.

Fireplace accessories—what is the total market? Percent breakdown by distribution outlet?

Provide a list of engineering companies that have merged with non-engineering companies within the past year.

Provide a list of a few books or articles on "American Depository Receipts." Also, a list of ten British companies for which ADR's are traded.

What is the base period for profit margin and the base period for dividends?

What states do not have an income tax?

Re: tuna and salmon. Pull together a complete profile on the industry and market. Who is involved, what processes are used, how distributed, history and myths; also information on tuna and salmon themselves.

Provide all demographic information on chain-saw users—who uses, where, how often?

How many new products and/or inventions come to the market each year? What percent succeed?

How are medicaid reimbursements made and what state/federal regulations are applicable in New Jersey, Arizona, Utah, Michigan, Idaho and California?

Provide the following information on opticians, optometrists, ophthalmologists and oculists. How many licensed in U.S.A.? What is the definition of each? Differences between each? How are pharmaceutical products distributed to these professions—particularly eye drops?

Obtain an article which appeared in the New York Times on gas mileage for various automobiles, stressing Mercedes Benz.

Obtain a list of books on the history of cordials and copy from five different encyclopedias what they have on the history of cordials.

The Indonesian government has new export regulations. What are they?

Provide data on R&D expenditures for ten major food companies.

Pricing trends in the shrimp industry. Are there any? If so, what?

How do you spell the actual sound the owl makes?

What is the cost of shipping 1000 lbs. of electronic hospital instruments from the U.S. to Hong Kong? How long would it take? What are the import/customs regulations?

How does reverse osmosis work?

Provide any articles since July 1975 on the business climate and opportunities in Brazil. Include a computer search.

Provide all available information on the medical and healthcare systems in the U.S.S.R. and the People's Republic of China.

What are the methods for forecasting agricultural commodity prices? Can you locate an expert on the subject?

Please obtain studies that have been done on the toxicity of benzoyl peroxide.

Do many supermarkets accept credit cards?

Who did—and please obtain—a report on the carcinogenic effects of tannic acid in tea?

Please obtain a list of New York's richest men.

What states have the ten lowest property taxes?

Is there any data on the use of corticosteroids in the treatment of sunburn? How many people need medical treatment for sunburn each year?

Who designed the L'eggs Panty Hose display rack?

Birth rate projections through 1985.

Could you provide a list of articles dealing with the effect of consumerism and ecology on soft drink packaging?

What amount of oil is needed for electricity to run New York City for one month? For one year?

Need names and addresses of four (4) marketing consultants to the black community.

What are the sales—in units and dollars—of the 10 major household appliances, by type?

Obtain articles about the most recent wine scandal in France.

What is the effect of clofibrate on blood cholesterol?

List of all foreign trade missions in the U.S. with addresses and phone numbers.

Please find us the article "Sugar and the New Theory about Heart Attacks."

What American or other European companies own substantial portions of A.E.G. Telefunken stock?

What percentage of people read books after they leave college?

Of those people who voted in 1976, what was their educational background by age group?

What is the cost and sweetening power of Xylitol?

Please find market share by manufacturer, on a dollar basis, of pet food market.

Bibliography on quackery; retrieve 6 or 7 recent survey articles on the devices and procedures currently being pushed.

Do computer search on "Children's Influence Concerning Purchase of Consumer Package Goods."

Microwave ovens—sales forecast, number in use, good background information, especially concerning impact on current food products.

Locate several places where oil shale projects are operating and get further details.

Do food additives have any known adverse effects on child development?

Who are the top ten national developers of: housing; commercial buildings; shopping areas; recreation and resort developments?

Who makes offshore drilling platforms that are not stationary? What is the future for these platforms?

ANY QUESTIONS?

CHAPTER 4

The Cost and Value of Information

The cost of anything is usually equated with the money needed to acquire it. But this is the consumer approach to cost. The business and professional approach equates cost to *value*. The value of information is equal to the *time and money* spent in acquiring it and the ultimate *profit* estimated from its use.

Time is the most precious thing we humans have in life. It is also the only finite thing we possess. No matter how we strive, we cannot increase it. No matter how much money we spend, how acquisitive we are, or how ingenious we get, we cannot gain more time.

So what is reasonable and what is expensive in assessing the cost of information must be considered in the light of these three factors: time, money, and ultimate gain.

Most information is already available—at a price. The majority of us have been conditioned to think that, because a public library is free, information is free. NO INFORMATION IS FREE. As students not involved in gainful employment, there was no cost factor when we spent our time at the library or anywhere else searching out information. But the moment we earn wages—working for ourselves or others—our time is worth money, and that same trip to the "free" library has a cost factor.

To repeat, information is not free. Information costs money—in dollars or time, or both. Information is probably the most *valuable* commodity available. But the cost of information is usually assessed falsely by the user, because most people have absolutely no conception of the amount of executive time, professional time, secretarial time, etc., which is spent in unearthing information about the external world. It makes no difference whether we are talking about important or unimportant information. Let us say that someone turns to a secretary and requests something as simple as, "I want to fly to San Francisco tomorrow. Please find out what flights and accommodations are available and make reservations for both." That secretary could spend at least two hours getting this information. With benefits, employer contributions, etc., obtaining that information could cost more than $30. Whereas, if the secretary—or executive or professional in the first instance—called a travel agent, the only cost would be for the initial call.

The primary reason that most people don't consider costs is that they don't think in terms of information. Instead, they think in terms of tasks, problems and questions.

It is incredible to realize the number of important, high-salaried people involved almost daily in the drudgery of gathering information of one type or another. Incredible because: (1) this information has been gathered before, and (2) this information is available at a price. If you have raised your level of information consciousness sufficiently to know these two things, you are already half-way towards answering your question; hence, *you have saved 50% of your time (money).* This is true because, when there is an information problem, 90% of the work is in finding the source and 10% of the work is in using the source material to get the answer.

Remember, too, that the value of information is in its application, not in the gathering of it.

Here is another reason for blockage to information consciousness. Most of us were reared with an absurd myth: You must do your own research to benefit knowledge-wise from the information gained (if you don't ask directions and you find your own way, you will learn better how to get there). Utter nonsense—and a sheer waste of time. Moreover, it is *inefficient.*

Trying to find the information on your own is also costly, as stated previously. In addition to the cost of your time as a professional, you must also add what is called the "opportunity cost." Let us assume that you are a consultant earning $50 per hour. If you do research or seek any information on your own, you would assume that this costs you $50 an hour. Right? Wrong! It costs you $100 an hour, because you are also losing one hour's worth of consulting income. And remember that it will probably take you twice as long to get the information as it might take a professional expert.

Now let's move from the cost of information to the *value.* THE VALUE OF ANY PIECE OF INFORMATION IS SUBJECTIVE. The same piece of information—let us assume a survey priced at $1,000—may be worth $10,000 to you, may be totally worthless to me, and may be worth exactly $1,000 to the next person.

Examples:

1.   The A.C. Nielsen Company does a continuous study which includes a measurement of the movement of different brands of corn flakes through supermarket outlets on a week-to-week and year-to-year comparative basis. This service sells for thousands of dollars per year. This study, needless to say, would be worthless to the owner of a "Mom & Pop" grocery store. It would be worth its price to a marketing consultant to the corn products industry. But it would be worth at least ten times its price to the Kellogg Company.

2.   The results of a survey done in October 1978 on the growth of the bottled water industry are available, let us say, for $100. The data is accurate and compiled by a reputable firm. But there is a problem. The bottled water industry has been growing by leaps and bounds since 1978, and much has changed radically. Because there has been no similar study since, your only alternative would be to conduct your own up-to-date survey at a cost of $10,000. What is the value of the $100-report? It would depend upon (a) whether you just have a passing interest in bottled water, (b) whether you intend to open a million-dollar bottled-water plant or (c) whether you are an advertising agency on the verge of making your pitch to a potential small account which bottles water. The $100-report is worthless to (a) because information must be acted upon to have value. It is also worthless to (b) because the information is too old on which to base a million-dollar expenditure. It has value to (c) as background material to impress the prospective client.

3.   Let's border on the science-fictional and assume that it would cost two million dollars to determine the number of bricks in all the buildings in Manhattan. Would anyone spend that kind of money for such seemingly worthless information? Yes—the used-brick dealer who was just

authoritatively informed by a seismologist that Manhattan will be totally destroyed by an earthquake in exactly ten months.

4. Back to mundane matters like "The Guide To Restaurants." The price of the book is $4. Would it pay to research the credentials of the author and the publisher? No, if you are only interested in it for one dinner. (Remember the value of time.) Yes, if you are a publisher contemplating issuing a competing book on that subject.

5. It minimally costs $75,00 per year to set up and maintain an in-house library. Is it worth it? You can answer the question yourself easily now by simply asking the appropriate successive question: *Worth it to whom?*

Information is one of the few commodities that ofttimes cannot be valued by price. This is because the benefits cannot always be measured in dollars. So if you do reach a high level of information consciousness and you happen to work for a large organization, be prepared for a fight with the comptroller when you request funds for information and do not offer an accurate dollar value in return. INFORMATION IS AN IMMEAS-URABLE INVESTMENT, Nevertheless, it *is* an *investment*, not a necessary evil tool. As a vital resource it should be considered in the same light as inventory or any other asset. But, like most assets, information is perishable, and it should be treated and regarded accordingly.

Perhaps in part because, as we have seen, the cost of information is difficult to define (how much is time worth?), the value of information is very subjective, and information itself is an intangible, many people confuse the value relationships involved. Either they believe they can get lots of information for little money, or little information for a lot of money. They ask a question which they believe will cost little to answer because the answer is of low value to them. Or they ask a question which they believe will cost a lot to answer because the answer is of high value to them. In fact, as often as not, the low value answer may cost a hundred times more to get than the high value answer.

How does the information conscious person deal with this problem? First, obviously, the fact is that you never make a firm assumption about how much you *think* it will cost to obtain whatever information you seek. Second, always be prepared to accept that the information you want may not be available to you at a price you can afford or are willing to pay.

Third—and most important—understand that virtually any question, any information problem, can be answered for $50, $500, $5,000 or $50,000 and more. It all depends on how much time is spent looking, how much depth and detail is required. This is one of the most important fundamental concepts in the information field, because it can help you scale the level and cost of the research to the value of the answer to *you*.

As an example, let's apply this concept to a specific problem and see what levels of information can be obtained, and for what situation each level is most appropriate.

Assume you are interested in a particular industry or market. It doesn't matter whether it's potato chips or glass or yoghurt. Here's a rough idea of what you might get at the various cost levels:

$50 - $100:

A few very broad statistics on the size of the market. Perhaps names of leading companies in the field. Useful when you need quick, general information.

$500 - $1,000:

Within this cost range, you should be able to get an overview of an industry based on a gathering of readily available secondary data. A reasonably comprehensive—but not exhaustive—search of published literature would be included. Major articles from trade journals, basic government statistics—essentially anything that has been collected and published. All of this could be useful for background information, speech-making, report writing, early stages of planning and problem-solving.

$5,000 - $10,000:

Based on the secondary information gathered above, plus more exhaustive searching and limited telephone contact with trade sources, a 20 to 100-page profile of an industry could be prepared for this cost range. It would cover the size of the market, companies in the field, distribution patterns, regulations, etc., though not with the depth and detail of the next level up. It would also be useful for the initial stages of studying an opportunity, a new product, a new venture or an acquisition.

$15,000 and up:

At this level, a full-scale industry and market study can be produced. It would include a fully exhaustive search of secondary data, extensive interviews with trade sources, manufacturers, retailers and other industry components; careful study of market potential and other factors affecting the industry—all embodied in a report, with summary and analysis, that might run up to several hundred pages. At the higher price ranges, a customized survey of consumers (whether individuals or other businesses) would be included. This type of in-depth study is essential for all advanced stages of planning, product introductions, acquisitions, etc.

Another way to perceive the cost-value problem is to look at the broad categories under which information can be obtained from the vast array of publishers and information-gathering organizations. The following are listed in order of least to most costly:

Published Information

This would include articles in the trade press, journals, collections of statistics, books, pamphlets, etc. Also data found through searching of computer data banks (See Chapter 7). This type of information is available through your own searching or through your use of librarians, researchers or information-retrieval companies.

Published Reports

Careful studies, usually with some analysis of some industry, technology or problem of wide commercial interest. The depth of the studies is analogous to the $5,000 to $10,000 level referred to earlier. However, because the publisher has financed the research and is selling the report in book form to many potential buyers, the cost of these published reports can be under $1,000.

Multi-Client Studies and Surveys

The subject matter and methodology used in completing these studies may closely resemble the Published Reports, though they are usually much more in depth. However, multi-client studies are "sponsored" in advance usually by a limited number of organizations. The sponsors can then request additional, highly specific questions they want answered as part of the study. This makes multi-client studies more useful for their needs than published studies. Typical prices paid by sponsors range from $2,000 to $10,000, but this is a fraction of what the full study would cost to contract for individually. In the case of consumer surveys, multi-client type studies are often referred to as "syndicated research."

Individually Contracted Studies and Surveys

These are ordered and paid for by a single entity, to whom the results belong exclusively. "Custom" studies and surveys of this kind may, of course, fall within a very broad price range, depending on the information needed.

The foregoing example should suggest points that cannot be repeated too often:

— Information that has already been published somewhere is much less expensive than information which must be gathered and developed on a customized basis.

— "Raw" information (a bunch of statistics from a book, copies of articles) is much less expensive to provide than any kind of written summary or report based on that information.

— In the case of large studies and surveys, it is always cheaper to purchase "off-the-shelf" than to contract for customized research.

— The more important the use to which the information will be put, the more exhaustive a research job should be done.

— Collecting secondary (published) information is much less costly than conducting primary, original research.

At this point you may say to yourself, "You've told me that information is not free, and you've told me something about its cost and value. But how do I know when it's really worth spending money for it?"

The answer is that you may never know, because the true value of information is often measured only in relation to the cost of the failure that results from not having it.

We once knew two salesmen who worked for the same company. They sold the same line of products to the same types of customers in similar territories. They both had the same background and experience.

Yet John, the first salesman, earned close to $50,000 a year, while Harry, the second, only managed to earn $25,000 a year. Harry was an excellent dresser, a smooth talker and a hard worker who wined and dined his customers regularly. He was, in fact, a good salesman. In an attempt to find out why John was twice as successful as Harry, the sales manager visited John at his home. There, in a basement office, was a veritable Library of Congress. There were complete files on each of John's customers. For each company, he had records on its history, earnings and plans. He had tearsheets of its advertising and notes on its marketing practices. He had information on each of his customer's problems. There was even a complete rundown on the executives he contacted within those companies—their hobbies, family, club memberships and the like. In short, John had a lot of information; Harry had very little. The information was worth $25,000 to John; the lack of it cost Harry at least $25,000.

A good way to measure the value of information (as promulgated by *Boardroom Reports*, May 15, 1976) is to make a comparison of "failure costs." For example, the likelihood of failure of a $100,000 project is one in three without research, so the failure cost is $33,000. With research, the risk of failure is one in five, for a failure cost of $20,000. The value of the research is then the difference between the two costs, or $13,000.

CHAPTER 5

Interpreting Information

In thinking back upon such business failures as the Edsel, it seems inconceivable to imagine that one of the largest manufacturing concerns in the world did not have sufficient information to prevent that debacle.

While we cannot say so with certainty (people are remarkably tight-lipped about failures) it is likely, on the contrary, that a very substantial amount of research was available to the automobile developers.

What went wrong, probably, was that the information on hand was improperly analyzed.

The causes of bad business decisions can be attributed, not only to a *lack* of information but also to the failure to properly *interpret* information.

Staying with the American automobile industry as an example, it lost twenty percent of its shares of market to foreign automakers by improperly interpreting its own consumer research. For many years, this research pointed up the fact that a large segment of the American consumers was seeking basic transportation rather than gussied-up gas-eaters. This segment did not look upon cars as status symbols. Having spent enormous amounts of money on research which gathered this kind of data, the Detroit executives interpreted this kind of information incorrectly. The result, as we know, has produced a disaster for our automotive industry and a bonanza for the foreign automakers.

Such failures can be significantly minimized if the information-conscious person will keep in mind that proper interpretation of information depends largely on the reliability of the source, the manner in which the information is presented, and the personal perception of the person receiving the information.

How reliable is the source? A seemingly simple question, seemingly simple to answer. Not at all.

Take supposedly "unimpeachable" sources, such as the annual *Statistical Abstract of the United States*, published by the U.S. Government and containing most of the key national population and other demographic statistics. A couple of years ago, the volume contained several vital number transposition errors! In fact, no source is unimpeachable. The main question is really whether it is the *only* source. If it is, then the data is as reliable as it can get. If it isn't, then a second source should be checked and is likely to produce a different set of data. For example, we have seen from different sources as many as a half-dozen different figures for the size of the fragrance industry in the U.S.

Another key issue is whether the source may have a bias, even one that may not be immediately recognized. As an illustration, the *New York Times* is considered an authoritative newspaper. Assume that it publishes a figure for U.S. sales of soft drinks in an article about Coca Cola. The figure may come to be taken as gospel and reprinted in other publications, even though the reporter writing the article may originally have obtained the figure from the National Soft Drink Association, which may well be a biased source. (Many associations publish figures about the size of their industry, and these are often the only figures available. Yet those figures often come from a poll of the association's members, who do not necessarily have the incentive to answer with complete candor.)

Is the information provided by the source up to date? Is it first-hand or second-hand? How did this source actually come up with this information? These are all primary issues that reflect on the reliability of the source. To take a very simple example: the recognized, authoritative source for demographic information is, of course, the U.S. Census. It is first-hand information, obtained through exhaustive survey procedures. (Though some have complained of undercounting.) Yet, the last census prior to publication of this book was completed in 1970, so the data, while from an authoritative source, is ten years old. Unfortunately, aside from periodic, limited updates and projections, there are no alternatives.

The manner in which information is presented when you receive it can significantly affect your use of it. Most information which has been assembled from statistics, data, facts, etc., has been "massaged" in some way before it gets to you. Massaging is the putting together of these elements in a manner which applies to a particular problem at hand. Let us assume that information concerning birth statistics in Indiana is required. Many different types of such statistics may be available from several different federal, state and local agencies. Gathering all of these statistics together, it may become necessary to create charts or graphs (or both) to make them intelligible. If ten people created charts from the same set of statistics, we would have ten different charts. This is because each person would "massage" the information in a different way. Yet all the different charts may be correct.

As another example, assume you wanted to know total dollar sales of widgets in the U.S. in 1978 and 1979. You might be shown a simple table like this:

1978	1979
$175,000,000	$195,000,000

Or, using the same data, you might be presented with a table like this:

	(millions of dollars)	
1978	1979	% Increase
175.0	195.0	+ 11.4

The second table would not only be easier to read, but presents more information using the exact same data. Reading the first table, you might quickly grasp that widget sales were up by $20 million, but you might miss the fact that the increase was only 11%; LESS than inflation.

Proper and accurate interpretation also depends upon your own abilities of perception. Always bear your original question in mind and pay close attention to such things as scales and legends on graphs and charts.

To continue our example, assume you commission a study of the widget industry. The researcher you assign to the project returns with a graphic representation of the trend in widget sales at the National Widget Company. Initially, you're not likely to pay too much attention to the scale on the graph. You'll look at it and see widget sales trending down slightly. A different researcher doing the same graph could use exactly the same data and present it on a graph with a different scale. Now you take a quick look at the graph and exclaim, "Widget sales are crashing!" The difference in your perception is caused by the scale of the graph.

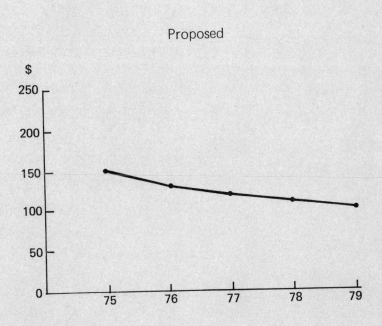

Proposed

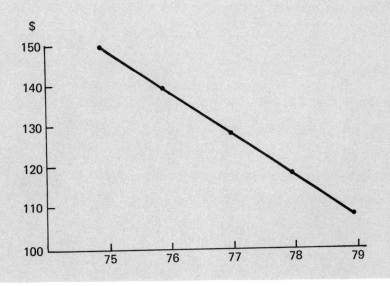

Your perception, therefore, should be based on the knowledge that people manipulate information to suit their purposes, or simply out of ignorance. Pay close attention.

Also, use your intelligence and common sense. Assume you wanted information on the defense electronics industry. You can't afford to commission a study, so you ask if one has been done and is available in published form to the public. You are delighted to be presented with the results of a study done in October, 1978. It is now March, 1980. A study may be only a year old. But, if you are reasonably well read, common sense would remind you that this particular industry changed radically in that year, so the survey results are of very limited value.

Above all, view all information with a bit of healthy skepticism. This is essential not because the information industry is overrun with charlatans and incompetents; it isn't. It is necessary because INFORMATION IS NOT AN EXACT SCIENCE.

And it never will be.

It may seem absurd to write this, but *unused* information is *useless*. A sourcebook never cracked is a waste. An encyclopedia bought and paid for is worthless if never referred to—as is any dictionary. But, it seems to us, it borders on the outrageous that so many professionals and business people subscribe to much-needed trade literature and even commission studies and surveys without ever glancing at them! Then there are those losers who read the information, but never use it. To be of value, information must be acted upon. If it is ignored, it is valueless. Too busy? If their competitors find time to take advantage of the world of information, those "too busy" people will soon find themselves with nothing to be busy about.

CHAPTER 6

The New Information Environment

The British are known for understatement, but we Americans are reared in an atmosphere of the overstated and the dramatic. What should be normal, expected growth or proliferation endemic to the evolution of our species and our brain is almost always described in revolutionary and explosive terms. The industrial *revolution*, the paperback *explosion*, the baby *boom*, the information *revolution*, the knowledge *explosion*. This is nonsense. We have naturally arrived at a point in our history toward which we have been headed all along; those with foresight are not at all surprised. And we shall continue to grow *exponentially* in every aspect of our society—for better or for worse.

In the case of information, it's time that we ceased experiencing "future shock" by recognizing the here-and-now, i.e. by raising our information consciousness. The best way to do this is to acquaint ourselves with and feel at home in our *new information environment.*

Information has, of course, been recorded, processed and distributed since the times when people were writing on stone and papyrus. Before our time in history, the single most significant event in the information business was the invention of the printing press, which enabled facts to be communicated to anyone at any place.

In the "olden days"—up until the middle of this century—people usually found information in any of three basic ways: by going to a library, by consulting a relatively limited number of reference books like encyclopedias and directories, or by using a handful of special services like Dun & Bradstreet's credit reporting service which was begun before 1900.

Then, in the mid-20th century, several developments combined to begin the creation of a new information environment.

First came the advent of the computer, which vastly increased the ability to store and process information.

Second, the launching of Sputnik generated a boom in technology, as well as a flurry of research activity. Scientific and technical information was produced in great quantity. Simultaneously, a society rapidly increasing in complexity created a thirst for knowledge, satisfied only in part by an astounding increase in the amount of published information. Indeed, the increase has been so exponential that we have been able to generate more printed information in the past ten years than in mankind's complete history! By one estimate, just the number of journal articles published in a year doubled between 1966 and 1974.

As the computer became more sophisticated (today's versions are 1000 times more powerful and 100,000 times less costly than the early models of the 1940's), as other communications technologies were perfected, and as information needs grew, a few forward-looking people began to think differently about the information environment.

Some began to see that libraries were not merely passive repositories for shelves of books, but could be more dynamic purveyors of knowledge. Some publishers began using computers to assist in the publication process, and realized they were not just in the publishing business, but in the information business. Suddenly, people began to realize that the value of technology would in fact be ultimately measured by the value of the information it helped to store and disseminate.

Significantly, in 1968 a group of companies including the likes of McGraw-Hill and Dun & Bradstreet formed the Information Industry Association, which has now grown to over 130 information-company members.

Gradually, elements of a new information environment were being put into place, and as the 1970's ended, they finally all came together—though still only dimly perceived by most people. The new environment is here, but few know it yet.

What are the particular characteristics of this new environment? First is the convergence of technologies in computers, communications and office automation. We have entered a world where satellites link computers together so they can "talk" to each other; where advances in voice and communications systems will allow meetings to be held by "teleconferencing;" where data can be "called up" on a television set; where general purpose computer terminals are located in millions of offices. Technology has come of age through integration. It is one thing to be able to use a computer to store lots of data; it is quite another thing when that computer can be linked to a communications system to transmit the data to remote locations.

Second, the new environment is characterized by a sudden surge in the availability of information, partly as a result of the advances in technology, but also because of demand. A sizeable portion of this demand has been caused by Washington's "need to know." The needs of the Federal Government have spawned a mountain of information collected and disseminated by Uncle Sam. The 1980 Census alone will involve hiring 275,000 workers, cost over $1 billion dollars and generate masses of data used both for critical political decisions such as the apportioning of the U.S. House of Representatives as well as for business and marketing purposes.

Underscoring the new interest in the availability of information was the passage of the Freedom of Information Act in 1966 (amended in 1974) designed to improve access to the millions of documents created by the Government. Today, some government agencies like the Food and Drug Administration are filling thousands of FOIA requests a year—mostly from businesses trying to get a better fix on their competition. The law even created dozens of service companies that help people obtain information from the Government bureaucracy.

The third characteristic of the new information environment is the astounding development of the information industry itself. Since the total amount of information available to us now doubles every ten years, it's no wonder we're no longer in a world where just a few publishers produce encyclopedias and almanacs. Instead, a vast network of information "manufacturers," "distributors" and "retailers" has evolved to collect, store, reformat, analyze, and disseminate data. Magazine publishers who were formerly traditional now produce "fact books" and collect and publish tons of data on the industries they cover. Multi-million dollar companies like A.C. Nielsen give us television ratings and also feed their computers with data on supermarket sales of peanut butter. Market research firms conduct surveys and polls using computerized techniques that make results instantly available. Literally hundreds of totally new directories and reference services appear every year—so many that we now have directories of directories, a newsletter on newsletters—even an information service on information services! In fact, the proliferation of sources and demand has created a new industry of information "retailers" or retrieval services that perform research on demand for people who don't have the time to cope with finding facts from among the dizzying array of possibilities. (More on these services later.)

But perhaps the most significant development has been the emergence of literally hundreds of computer data banks that are rapidly creating completely new approaches in the way we can obtain information. We will examine these in depth in the next chapter.

The fourth characteristic of the new information environment is the rise of the information professional—the individual who knows how to "manage" the collection, retrieval and use of information . . . who will make sense out of it all. These new professionals are something of a hybrid: librarian, records manager, data processing manager and researcher. In fact, many are getting their titles changed to "information manager" (a new magazine by that name was recently started), and some companies are appointing high-level officers to information management positions with responsibility not only for data processing, but for office automation, the library, research, communications and other information-related functions. One futurist has predicted that the so-called "Vice President of Information Resources" will soon be the most coveted position in a company.

The new information environment we're describing has emerged so quickly, that few have learned how to use it. Yet it is already changing the way sophisticated companies and executives do business. Here are a few "tip-of-the-iceberg" glimpses of what this new information environment means:

— If you want to know what's been written about something, the fact that it can probably be found is not so far-fetched when you realize that a summary of virtually every major article in the business press published in the past five years is stored on computer and readily retrievable in the space of a few minutes.

— If you are an industrial marketer, you can now get county-by-county industrial purchasing potential estimates and plant locations by size and industry.

— If you sell to consumers, there is a wealth of consumer purchasing power statistics readily available, including a myriad of breakdowns by zip code.

— When you need information on publicly held companies, you can get it from reports filed with the Securities and Exchange Commission. These reports are now indexed and available on microfiche or from dozens of new service firms that have suddenly appeared to retrieve them for you.

— Government information dissemination capabilities have expanded almost beyond reason. Are you interested in overseas markets? There's a U.S. government expert for virtually every nation in the world, and you can call him or her on the phone. In fact, market profiles by industry are often available for nearly any country you can think of.

— Are you looking for new suppliers overseas or keeping tabs on competitive importers? There's a computerized service that keeps track of imports into the U.S. for various commodities by country and port of origin, port of arrival and consignee!

— Interested in how your company is doing in terms of key measurements of performance like earnings as a percentage of sales, or earnings per share, or assets to liabilities? Computerized services exist that will compare your results to as many publicly held companies in as many industries as you like.

— Want to pinpoint your marketing? Simply select the industry you market to, the size of the company that makes the best customer, the title of your typical buyer, the zip codes where you'd like to sell. A printout of prospective customers' names can be on your desk in days.

— Want to know who is selling the most potato chips in supermarkets and how much they sell? The question is no longer whether you can get this information, but rather whether you would like it nationally or regionally; ranked by units or dollars.

That's the tip of the iceberg. Now let's take a look at the iceberg itself.

But before we do, consider this. A number of people have already acclimatized themselves to the new information environment, and they are taking full advantage of it to improve their *personal* lives. They wear pieces of microfilm to describe their medical condition; they constantly check ahead for weather and traffic information; they use library information and referral services; they use home computers for appointment schedules, educational material, personal finances, list-keeping, reminders and other informational requirements. How far behind, then, are the executives, business people, consultants and other professionals who are not taking advantage of our new information environment *to earn their livelihoods?*

CHAPTER 7

The Computer Data Bank

The key to the new information environment described in the previous chapter is the computer data bank. Strangely enough, we use computer data banks all the time, but we just don't look at them as such. Telephone books, directories of all kinds, some catalogues and even airline and bus schedules are actually data banks in published form. The stock market listing is a data bank published daily.

Of course, if you're looking for information, the traditional ways of looking for it—in libraries, microfilm files, indices, encyclopedias—may still be valid. But often they are not updated frequently enough for your needs. Or they don't cover enough ground. So the information you get may not be appropriate because it may be dated or incomplete.

What's more, as information begins to pile up, the specific information we need must be located within millions and millions of items. It's like looking for the proverbial needle in a haystack. This can be too costly, too time-consuming or even virtually impossible for you and/or your staffs to find.

Enter the computer data bank.

Planning Review had an excellent article called "Welcome to the Information Revolution," and we have incorporated some of its concepts in this chapter.

We've all heard about the magical information bank of the future that contains all the answers to everybody's questions. For the moment, this is still very much a myth. But what we have instead are hundreds of individual information banks that collectively add up to almost the same thing.

The age of data banks is now here. The age of poring through piles of books in the library is now over.

What exactly is a computer data bank? A data bank (or data base, as it is commonly called) is quite simply a storage place for information. Each individual bank is a file of information on a subject or family of subjects that is stored and maintained in a computer's memory. The speed of the computer enables users to refer to any item in the file within seconds or minutes.

Some data bases are bibliographic, storing references to and summaries of articles in periodicals, journals, newspapers and the like. For example, a brief abstract of every article published in the *New York Times* is stored in a data base called The New York Times Information Bank.

Other data bases store an incredible amount of statistical data, such as demographic statistics, econometric data, stock and bond prices, buying power information and the like. For instance, the U.S. Prices Data Bank (available through Data Resources, Inc.) stores consumer, wholesale and industrial price indices compiled by the Bureau of Labor Statistics. The Value Line data base (maintained by Arnold Bernhard & Co.) stores financial data on 14,000 U.S. firms.

Still other data bases keep track of things like foundation grants, research in process, patents, available technology, and government documents. For example, a data base called CIS INDEX (produced by Congressional Information Services) covers U.S. Congress publications, hearings, House and Senate reports, etc.

Some particularly sophisticated—and expensive—data bases specialize in forecasting and allow you to perform correlations and analyses. Users tied into time-sharing computer programs can perform calculations using the data stored in the file. Or, they can input their own data to the computer in order to make comparisons. Some data banks include complex econometric models that enable users to measure alternatives through mathematical simulations.

There are now thousands of different data bases in existence and the number is growing daily. Several hundred of these are available to the public, with literally millions of items of information readily retrievable by anyone with a computer terminal.

The data bases are created and maintained by a wide variety of organizations, big and small, public and private . . . like the New York Times, or Predicasts, or the National Library of Medicine. Many of them have only become available since the mid 1970's.

Data bases, as mentioned above, are available to you through common computer terminals that connect to a telephone. Access to the data bases is offered by what are called on-line information systems, or vendors. Through a terminal, you can "dial-up" a system that offers one or more data bases. In a sense, these systems are "distributors" that have obtained their files from the data-base producers. (Some vendors are also producers of their own data bases.)

Looking for information in a data bank is called a search. To perform a search, someone sits at a terminal, dials an on-line system and selects the individual data base or bases to be searched. To ask the particular data bank chosen for information, you enter an appropriate set of terms and, in a matter of minutes, the computer will respond with an answer that appears on the terminal screen (if it has one) or in a printout, or both. The typical printout will show either the series of statistics requested or, in the case of bibliographic data bases, information about published articles on the subject, including brief abstracts or summaries.

The world of commercially available on-line information systems is just a few years old. But it has already dramatically changed the way many leading corporations and sophisticated information users gather data. It has been estimated that in 1965 there were probably fewer than 20 data bases available to the public for information retrieval purposes. By 1980 there were more than 300. In 1965, perhaps a few thousand people had performed searches on data bases. In 1975, almost a million on-line searches were performed. By 1985, the number of searches is expected to exceed 20 million.

Searching for information by computer enables you to find, in minutes, what formerly would have taken you hours, perhaps days. For example, an accomplished librarian's average time for a manual search of the published literature on a subject might be 3.5 hours, whereas the same search on a single data base can yield better results in five minutes. The results will be better because in that space of time the computer can search through millions of items.

Data bases are not only *fast.* They are *thorough.* We recently searched one data base to find articles written on the subject of corn and found references to 7,270 items on that subject. Fortunately, however, data bases are also *versatile* in that they enable you to limit your search to come up with just those few items that match your specific needs.

Now, at this point, you might be saying to yourself, "Okay, data banks sound great, but what do they mean to *me*?"

What they mean to you can be summarized in two very simple rules of thumb:

(1) Frequently, gaining knowledge means finding out quickly what has been written about an industry, a product, a company, a management technique, an individual, a place—anything. Data bases can tell you what's been published about almost anything in minutes.

(2) At other times, gaining knowledge means that you need some hard statistics. Data banks can be used to retrieve an enormous amount of collected information, ranging from census data to patent data to government statistics to financial data to facts on foundation grants.

Keeping these two rules in mind will suggest the versatility of present-day data banks and their direct usefulness to you.

Every day, more and more professionals, students, congressmen, librarians, consultants and business executives plug into computers to gather information for planning, marketing, technical research and general decision-making purposes. The White House routinely distributes printouts from commercially available data bases.

Let's take just a handful of typical problems and see how they can be solved using some of these data banks.

You've received a call from the Brazilian embassy informing you that a major Brazilian industrialist has arrived in the U.S. and has expressed a special interest in your products. He wants to visit you the day after tomorrow. You know very little about Brazil and, therefore, need a quick rundown of recent economic, political and social developments in that country. Using a data base like The New York Times Information Bank can make you a virtual expert in a few minutes time.

```
BRAZILIAN STATISTICS SHOW 12% DECLINE IN AGRI-
CULTURAL OUTPUT IN SOUTH-CENTRAL BRAZIL IN '78,
RAISING DOUBTS ABOUT PRELIMINARY '78 GROSS
DOMESTIC PRODUCT {GDP} GROWTH RATE FIGURE OF
6.3%; GDP BREAKDOWN SHOWS INDUSTRIAL GROWTH OF
8.6%, SERVICES GROWTH OF 6.1% AND AGRICULTURAL
PRODUCT OF MINUS 1.8%; CENTRAL-SOUTH BRAZIL
ACCOUNTS FOR 85% OF TOTAL AGRICULTURAL OUTPUT,
THEREFORE PRODUCTION IN NORTHEAST MUST HAVE
INCREASED BY 56% TO PRODUCE OVERALL DECLINE
FIGURE OF 1.8% {S}
   LATIN AMERICAN ECONOMIC REPORT   JANUARY 19, 1979
      PAGE: 21  COLUMN: 3

MIAMI HERALD SURVEY OF '78 ECONOMIC GROWTH IN
LATIN AMERICA AND CARIBBEAN AREA FINDS PARAGUAY
HAD HIGHEST GROWTH RATE OF 9.5%, WHILE ARGENTINA,
PERU, GUYANA AND JAMAICA HAD DECLINES IN GROWTH,
AND NICARAGUA, BESET BY POLITICAL TURMOIL, HAD
ZERO GROWTH RATE; NOTES PARAGUAY IS ENJOYING BOOM
BASED ON AGRICULTURAL EXPORTS AND JOINT CON-
STRUCTION WITH BRAZIL OF HUGE, ITAIPU HYDRO-
ELECTRIC DAM; DISCUSSES IMPACT OF US RECESSION ON
LATIN AMERICA, NOTING INFLATION AND DOLLAR DECLINE
HELP FORCE UP WORLD'S INTEREST RATES, THUS
DEPRESSING LATIN AMERICAN ECONOMIES WITH THEIR
HEAVY FOREIGN DEBTS; NOTES US ECONOMIC DECLINE
ALSO REDUCES US IMPORTS FROM LATIN AMERICA; MAP
OF LATIN AMERICA AND CARIBBEAN AREA; CHARTS OF
'77-'78 ECONOMIC GROWTH RATES {L}
   MIAMI HERALD                      JANUARY 15, 1979
      PAGE: 1  COLUMN: 6
```

EXPLORATION AND EXPLOITATION OF BRAZIL'S VAST
AMAZON BASIN BY MULTI-NATIONAL COMPANIES AND
BRAZILIAN GOVERNMENT IS REVEALING INCREDIBLE
WEALTH IN NATURAL RESOURCES; INTERIOR BRAZIL MAY
HOLD 10,000 TONS OF GOLD, $1 TRILLION WORTH OF
TIMBER AND UNLIMITED RESERVES OF IRON, TIN AND
BAUXITE; MINING AND TIMBER OPERATIONS SPREADING
THROUGHOUT AMAZON BASIN POSE GROWING ENVIRONMENTAL
DANGER TO AREA, WHICH IS ONE OF MOST ECOLOGICALLY
FRAGILE REGIONS ON EARTH; UNRESTRAINED EXPLOITA-
TION COULD TIP BALANCE AND TURN LAND OF NATURAL
TREASURE INTO BARREN WASTELAND; BRAZILIAN GOVERN-
MENT'S CHIEF AIM IS TO HARVEST AND EXPORT VAST
TIMBERLAND TO ALLEVIATE BRAZIL'S STAGGERING
FOREIGN DEBT AND TRADE DEFICIT; HOSTILE CONDITIONS
ENCOUNTERED BY WORKERS IN AMAZON BASIN DESCRIBED;
VARIOUS DEVELOPMENT PROJECTS NOTED; PHOTOS {L}
   NEWSWEEK   JANUARY 15, 1979
      PAGE: 67 COLUMN: 1

EDWIN MCDOWELL EXAMINES BRAZIL'S INTERNATIONAL
TRADE POLICIES AND NOTICES SIGNS THAT BRAZIL IS
EMERGING AS WORLD POWER; FOCUSES ON DIVERSIFICA-
TION OF EXPORTS AS MILITARY GOVERNMENT'S GUIDING
MAXIM TO AVOID DEPENDENCY ON A FEW CROPS, SUCH AS
COFFEE, AND ON LARGE TRADING PARTNERS, ESPECIALLY
US; NOTES THAT EXPORTS OF AGRICULTURAL PRODUCTS,
WHILE LARGE, HAVE DROPPED TO 48.7% OF EXPORTS IN
'77 FROM 65.5% IN '70; DETAILS COUNTRY'S BLATANTLY
PROTECTIONIST POLICIES THAT INCLUDE HEAVY
SUBSIDIES, TAX INCENTIVES TO PRODUCE EXPORTABLE
COMMODITIES, RESTRICTIONS ON MULTINATIONAL COM-
PANIES DOING BUSINESS IN BRAZIL, DOMINANT GOVERN-
MENT ROLE IN COMPANIES, IMPORT AND CURRENCY CURBS
AND UNWILLINGNESS TO PAY FOR TECHNOLOGY EXCEPT IN
JOINT VENTURES THAT FAVOR BRAZIL'S INTERESTS;
PHOTO OF TEXTILE FACTORY AND '70-'78 CHART OF
YEARLY EXPORTS COMPARING AGRICULTURAL AND NON-
AGRICULTURAL PRODUCTS {M}
   NEW YORK TIMES   JANUARY 7, 1979
     SECTION: 3 PAGE: 1 COLUMN: 1 FICHE: 7-04-1

```
BRAZILIAN ECONOMY MINISTER MARIO SIMONSEN
ESTIMATES OVERALL '79 GROWTH AT 5%; SIMONSEN
FORECASTS INDUSTRIAL GROWTH RATE OF 7.5%; BLAMES
LOW GROWTH IN AGRICULTURAL SECTOR ON DROUGHTS IN
SOUTHERN BRAZIL {S}
    LATIN AMERICAN ECONOMIC REPORT   JANUARY 5, 1979
      PAGE: 6  COLUMN: 3
```

```
BRAZIL REPORTS THAT ITS '78 INFLATION RATE REACHED
40.8%, 2 PERCENTAGE POINTS ABOVE '77; INFLATION
ROSE 1.5% IN DEC, BRINGING TOTAL RATE FOR YEAR TO
40.8%, UP FROM 38.8% IN '77 {S}
    NEW YORK TIMES                   JANUARY 4, 1979
      SECTION: 4  PAGE: 4  COLUMN: 6  FICHE: 4-79-15
```

Now you're working for a consumer products company, planning the expansion of Aunt Mama's Frozen Pizza. It's been selling well in the East, and the time has come to expand. You're thinking about test marketing in a couple of supermarkets in Phoenix, and you need a quick look at the demographics of the population living near those particular supermarkets. If you'll accept a single page printout within the hour at a cost of less than $100, a data base called SITE (produced by C.A.C.I.) can give you a detailed summary picture for as wide an area around the supermarkets as you choose. Included will be population, households, family income, and household income. Here's a sample of the type of printout you can get:

INCOME FORECAST REPORT

PHOENIX SMSA   LATITUDE: 0   0   0
ANY AREA IN USA   LONGITUDE: 0   0   0
ANY SIZE OR SHAPE   SPECIFIC INCLUSIONS ONLY

                                                    WEIGHTING   100.0

	1979 (EST.)	1980 FORECAST	1985 FORECAST	1980-1985 CHANGE	ANNUAL GROWTH
POPULATION	1329303	1362917	1511178	148261	2.1%
HOUSEHOLDS		472193	518640	46447	1.9%
FAMILIES		332649	364139	31490	1.8%
AVG HH SIZE		2.9	2.9	0.0	0.2%
AVG FAM SIZE		3.2	3.3	0.0	0.2%
TOT INC {MIL$}		9226.6	12256.5	3029.9	5.8%
PER CAPITA INC	$ 6769	$ 8110	$ 1341	3.7%

- -

	1979 (EST.)	%	1980 FORECAST	%	1985 FORECAST	%
FAMILY INCOME						
$ 0- 4999	21533	6.6	19223	5.8	9780	2.7
$ 5000- 6999	18126	5.6	16590	5.0	9558	2.6
$ 7000- 9999	24917	7.7	22310	6.7	11512	3.2
$ 10000-14999	64368	19.8	61503	18.5	43973	12.1
$ 15000-24999	131453	40.4	140064	42.1	172494	47.4
$ 25000-49999	50372	15.5	56599	17.0	90941	25.0
$ 50000 UP	14607	4.5	16360	4.9	25881	7.1
TOT NO. FAMILIES	325376	100.0	332649	100.0	364139	100.0
AVG FAM INC	$ 20202		$ 21077		$ 25106	
MEDIAN FAM INC	$ 17567		$ 18334		$ 21217	
HOUSEHOLD INCOME						
$ 0- 4999	42414	9.2	37645	8.0	18663	3.6
$ 5000- 6999	34041	7.4	32141	6.8	21745	4.2
$ 7000- 9999	43691	9.5	40537	8.6	25145	4.8
$ 10000-14999	94933	20.6	92856	19.7	74834	14.4
$ 15000-24999	165461	35.8	177640	37.6	228049	44.0
$ 25000-49999	63008	13.7	71130	15.1	117444	22.6
$ 50000 UP	18004	3.9	20244	4.3	32760	6.3
TOT NO. HH	461552	100.0	472193	100.0	518640	100.0
AVG HH INC	$ 18677		$ 19540		$ 23632	
MEDIAN HH INC	$ 15949		$ 16853		$ 20215	

- -

IMPORTANT: HOUSEHOLD INCOME INCLUDES THE INCOME OF FAMILIES AND
            UNRELATED INDIVIDUALS. HOUSEHOLD INCOME IS THE TOTAL
            AVAILABLE INCOME IN THE AREA.
- -

SOURCE: CACI,ARLINGTON,VIRGINIA
             LOS ANGELES, CALIFORNIA

COPYRIGHT 1979 CACI, INC.-FEDERAL

Perhaps you need to know unit sales of microwave ovens for the past year, and the outlook for next year. If this question had occurred to you at the end of 1979, a quick search of the PROMPT data base produced by a company called Predicasts would have yielded dozens of items on the subject. Here are just three:

```
4/4/1
514138  WSJ {SPR}  79/11/05  P16
   COMPUTER CHIP SHORTAGES ARE HOLDING BACK
PRODUCTION FOR MANY USERS. MILTON BRADLY CO'S BIG
TRACK ELECTRONIC TOY, DESIGNED TO SWEEP THE
CHRISTMAS MARKET, COULD BE SET BACK A YEAR WITHOUT
THE NECESSARY ICS. STANLEY WORKS HAS PUT OFF
PRODUCING A NEW AUTOMATIC GARAGE OPENER BECAUSE
OF THE SHORTAGE. RAYTHEON CO'S AMANA DIV REPORTS
THAT COMPONENT SHORTFALLS HAVE MADE THE PROJECTION
OF MICROWAVE OVEN SALES DIFFICULT, CAUSING THE
FIRM TO LENGTHEN ITS FORECAST SCOPE FROM 3 MOS TO
6 MOS. MOTOROLA INC VP CE THOMPSON SAYS THAT
SUPPLIERS ARE TRYING THEIR BEST TO KEEP UP WITH
USER DEMAND, BUT 1979'S SUDDEN JUMP IN ORDERS,
PARTICULARLY FROM SMALL FIRMS JUST STARTING TO
USE ICS IN PRODUCTS, EXCEEDS PRODUCTION CAPACITY.


4/4/2
515666  MART  79/11  P35
   US MICROWAVE OVEN AND RANGE RETAIL SALES IN
1980 SHOULD BE UP 15% FROM 1979'S 2.75 MIL
UNITS, ACCORDING TO LITTON MICROWAVE COOKING
PRODUCTS {MINNEAPOLIS, MINN} PRES W BLEDSOE.
```

```
4/4/3
514385  MERCH MO  79/11  P40
   US COOKING SALES {000 UNITS}
   PRODUCT                     1978     1979    % 79/78
   ELECTRIC RANGES            3,218    3,091    - 3.9
      FREE-STANDING           2,337    2,254    - 3.6
      BUILT-IN                  881      837    - 5.0
   GAS RANGES                 1,797    1,876    + 4.4
      FREE-STANDING/SET-IN    1,545    1,616    + 4.6
      HIGH OVEN                 123      129    + 4.9
      BUILT-IN                 129      131    + 1.6
   SMOOTHTOP RANGES            249      218    -12.4
   MICROWAVE OVENS            2,422    2,711    +11.9
      COUNTERTOP              2,190    2,425    +10.7
      COMBINATION              232      286    +23.3
   SOURCE:   MERCHANDISING'S 5TH    ANNUAL    MAJOR
   APPLIANCE   STATISTICAL  &  MARKETING    REPORT


   4/4/4
   515284  ELEC NEWS  79/10/29  PIS
     DESPITE AN UNSTEADY ECONOMY, MICROWAVE OVEN
   MANUFACTURERS ARE PREDICTING THAT SALES WILL RISE
   10% OR MORE THROUGH 1980. THEY CITE THE STRENGTH
   OF SALES THROUGH 9.5 MOS IN 1979, IN THE FACE OF
   DOUR PREDICTIONS ON THE ECONOMY AS A POINT IN
   FAVOR OF SALES CONTINUING. THE MARKET FOR COUNTER-
   TOP MICROWAVE UNITS WILL GROW THROUGH 1979 IN THE
   FOLLOWING WAYS: AS SUPPLEMENTARY UNITS TO CON-
   VENTIONAL RANGES NOW IN HOMES; AS PART OF A
   MODULAR KITCHEN CONCEPT REPLACING THE TOP BAKE
   OVEN IN BUILT-INS BECAUSE OF THE INCREASE IN
   REMODELING; AND ALL-IN-ONE MICROWAVE/ELECTRIC OR
   GAS RANGE COMBINATIONS AS A REPLACEMENT UNIT FOR
   OLDER RANGES. MANUFACTURERS POINT TO LITTON
   MICROWAVE DIV'S INCREASED PRODUCTION CAPACITY OF
   ABOUT 40% TO MORE THAN 1 MIL UNITS/YR AND TAPPAN
   CO'S 3+ MIL UNITS/YR LEVEL AS EXAMPLES OF PRODUCT
   RELIABILITY.
```

The above items show summaries of reported figures in trade periodicals from late 1979. Not only can you see unit sales of microwave ovens for

1978 *and* 1979, but you also have a leading manufacturer's forecast of the projected 1980 increase, as well as a trade periodical's forecast, which is slightly different. In addition, the data show that Litton's estimate of 1979 unit sales is slightly different from *Merchandising* magazine's estimate. As an added benefit, the printout gives you a general comparison of microwave unit sales with other cooking appliances.

You're suddenly given the task of helping the sales manager of an industrial products company plan the development of sales territories, estimate sales potential in each area and provide the sales staff with better leads. If the product can be classified using a four-digit SIC (Standard Industrial Classification) code, your task can be virtually complete in a day. A data base maintained by Economic Information Systems, Inc. will give you the estimated market for your product by state, county and individual buying plant—in other words, your market potential by territory and your list of prospects. The same data base, incidentally, can be used to discover such wonderful things as the size and market share of companies and individual plants, sales of privately held companies, and manufacturing facilities of large organizations. For example, here's the printout showing the names, location and addresses of the Midland Glass Company's major plants. Included is each plant's estimated dollar volume, employment and share of the market.

```
PRINT 1/5/1-5
DIALOG FILE 22: EIS PLANTS NOV79 {TYPES $0.50
EACH} {COPR. EIS INC.}
{ITEM   1 OF   5} USER 470 28JAN80

145735
   MIDLAND GLASS COMPANY
      2300 S 3RD BOX 2127
      TERRE HAUTE, INDIANA 47802
      COUNTY : VIGO
      812-234-6678
```

3221 GLASS CONTAINERS

SALES MIL $: 030.2   INDUSTRY % : 0.81
EMPLOYMENT : 5 {250-499}

 MIDLAND GLASS CO INC 09882 * PUBLIC
   CLIFFWOOD AVE
   CLIFFWOOD, NEW JERSEY 07721 201-566-4000

144125
  MIDLAND GLASS CO INC
   CLIFFWOOD AVE
   CLIFFWOOD, NEW JERSEY 07721
   COUNTY : MONMOUTH
   201-566-4000

   3221 GLASS CONTAINERS

   SALES MIL $: 052.9   INDUSTRY % : 01.42
   EMPLOYMENT : 6 {500-999}

 MIDLAND GLASS CO INC 09882 * PUBLIC
   CLIFFWOOD AVE
   CLIFFWOOD, NEW JERSEY 07721 201-566-4000

124021
  MIDLAND GLASS CO INC
   P O BOX 69
   SHAKOPEE, MINNESOTA   55379
   COUNTY : SCOTT

   612-445-5000

   3221 GLASS CONTAINERS

   SALES MIL $: 017.0   INDUSTRY % : 0.46
   EMPLOYMENT : 4 {100-249}

 MIDLAND GLASS CO INC 09882 * PUBLIC
   CLIFFWOOD AVE
   CLIFFWOOD, NEW JERSEY 07721 201-566-4000

```
MIDLAND GLASS CO INC
   BOLLINGER RD
   HENRYETTA, OKLAHOMA 74437
   COUNTY :   OKMULGEE
   918-652-9631

   3221 GLASS CONTAINERS

   SALES MIL $ :   022.7   INDUSTRY % :   0.61
   EMPLOYMENT :   5 {250-499}

MIDLAND GLASS CO INC   09882 * PUBLIC
   CLIFFWOOD AVE
   CLIFFWOOD, NEW JERSEY 07721   201-566-4000


020629
MIDLAND GLASS CO INC
   INDUSTRIAL PK/BOX 2127
   WARNER ROBINS, GEORGIA 31093
   COUNTY :   HOUSTON
   912-922-4271

   3221 GLASS CONTAINERS

   SALES MIL $ :   017.3   INDUSTRY % :   0.47
   EMPLOYMENT :   4 {100-249}

MIDLAND GLASS CO INC   09882 * PUBLIC
   CLIFFWOOD AVE
   CLIFFWOOD, NEW JERSEY 07721   201-566-4000
```

Amazing, isn't it?

A word about the SIC code, its origin and use. The SIC code was originally developed by the Government to facilitate collection and presentation of data on industries. The SIC assigns each business establishment a four-digit industry code based on its primary activity which is determined by the principal product produced or distributed or service rendered. A manufacturer with an SIC of 3561, for example, is in the non-electrical machinery business (35), making general industrial machinery (356) and specifically pumps and pumping equipment (3561).

The SIC code is critically important because all Census industry statistics are organized by SIC number, and because the SIC scheme has been very widely adopted by non-government information sources.

The manual that is the guide to the SIC scheme and lists what types of businesses are included within each SIC number is:

Standard Industrial Classification Manual
U.S. Office of Management and Budget
Executive Office of the President
U.S. Government Printing Office

No business should be without one.

Actually, the list of possible uses of data bases is virtually endless.

— Do you need to know what new technology is available for energy conservation in industrial plants? What lessons are to be learned from other companies' experiences in hiring energy consultants? That's easy work for a data bank called ENERGYLINE.

— Do you need to find a study on the computer market in Mexico? That's in a data base called NTIS.

— Would you like background information on ozone generation in the atmosphere of Los Angeles? Mere child's play for a data base called ENVIROLINE.

— What's new in packaging methods for soft drinks? PIRA can handle that one.

- What's new in the area of corporate image advertising? The IN-FORM and MANAGEMENT CONTENTS data bases can give you scores of examples.

- Developing trends in surgicenters? That's in MEDLINE.

- A list of patents owned by the National Can Corporation? Try CLAIMS.

- Up-to-the-minute news about your competitors, or about your own company? That's readily available from the Dow Jones News Retrieval System.

And that is only a glance at the iceberg. Entire directories exist (see the Appendix) that tell you all about the hundreds of available data bases and what they contain.

There are two ways you can use data banks and get the results of on-line searching.

The first way is to get your own computer terminals and obtain access to the major on-line systems and data bases. The terminals, which can include either or both a video and print unit, generally cost between $150 and $400 a month. The individual data bases then invoice you monthly for the search time you actually use. That charge generally varies between $0.75 and $3.00 per minute. Some data bases, especially those associated with econometric and financial data-base modeling, require you to pay an annual access fee, which can run to tens of thousands of dollars.

Most data banks also offer or require a formal training program which can cost a few hundred dollars.

You also have to train searchers to operate your terminals and become familiar with the capabilities of the various data bases. One word of caution:

You must use the data bases continually or you'll get rusty from lack of practice. That increases your cost per search.

The second way to access computer data banks is to avoid having any terminals of your own and instead go to a "retailer" or information retrieval service. These companies have their own terminals already hooked up to many of the available data bases and will perform individual searches on order. All you have to do is ask the question. The retailers will plan and execute the search, select the appropriate data bases to use and deliver the results to you, generally within one to ten days. (If you have a terminal, arrangements can be made for a retailer to perform the search and have the results delivered on your terminal.)

Retailers' fees range between $20 and $75 per hour, plus the cost of the actual computer time used. (For a representative list of retailers see the Appendix.)

The advantages of using retailers are, of course, that you don't pay any fixed costs or worry about training, and you do not need access to a large number of different data bases. Further, most retailers are highly proficient searchers and they usually offer related research services. (See Chapter 8)

The major disadvantages are that you pay the retailer's fee and mark-up and you must wait for delivery of your printout. In addition, retailers generally do not offer searches on data bases that charge large access fees.

Many companies are now combining use of their own terminals with use of outside retailers. They use their own terminals for frequently searched data bases and ask retailers to search data bases not directly accessed or infrequently used.

There are two drawbacks (if such they can be called) to data bases:

(1) If you want to see the full text of an article cited or summarized

by a data base, you must retrieve it from the original source, consult a library or otherwise find it. This problem has caused the emergence of so-called document retrieval firms that will retrieve on request copies of articles, pamphlets, books, etc. Prices for retrieving an article average around $6 to $7. In the future, it is likely that this drawback will be somewhat alleviated by the emergence of full-text data bases.

(2) Data banks cannot solve all your problems or answer all your questions. They cannot perform magic. Despite tantalizing articles slanted toward the dramatic, and despite the claims of advertising, ALL INFORMATION IS NOT AVAILABLE IN DATA BANKS, and never will be. There is a monumental amount of it, but not *all.* The computer is a very finite, logical instrument. It regurgitates what is put into it. Since we cannot put all knowledge in, we cannot get all knowledge out. Often, false assumptions (again) are made. Suppose you know about the demographic profile available in the SITE data base, a sample of which we showed you earlier. It contains information on households with televisions, washers, air conditioners, etc. You cannot assume from this that it also contains information on households with radios. It doesn't.

But these minor limitations cannot hold a candle to the prodigious amounts of information that data banks *do* have. We've talked about lots of different data bases. Here are examples of just five and what they contain:

NTIS

This data base contains citations of over 500,000 publicly available reports on research projects sponsored by federal agencies and some state and local governments. Produced by the National Technical Information

Service, the data base is a cross-disciplinary one with items dating back to 1964.

PREDICASTS F&S INDEXES

Prepared by Predicasts, Inc., this data base contains over 1.5 million records dating back to 1972. It covers domestic and international company, product and industry information. The data base contains citations from over 2,500 publications and includes information on corporate acquisitions and mergers, new products, technological developments and socio-political factors.

ERIC

Prepared by the Education Resources Information Center, this is a complete data base on journals, reports and projects in the field of education. It contains over 330,000 records dating back to 1966.

TOXLINE

This data base contains information on published human and animal toxicity studies, effects of environmental chemicals and pollutants and adverse drug reactions. It has nearly a million records dating as far back as 1950. It is produced by the National Library of Medicine.

TECHNOTEC

Designed to promote technology transfer, this data base contains details about available technologies submitted by companies, agencies, and universities internationally. Users can search for technologies or submit their own for inclusion. Produced by Control Data, Technotec contains about 25,000 records from 1975 on.

INFORMATION BANK

This data base contains citations and abstracts of nearly 2 million articles from the *New York Times* and over 60 other newspapers and periodicals. It is prepared by the *New York Times* and includes items dating back to 1969.

So much for a look at the iceberg itself.

CHAPTER 8

Rx for Information Paralysis

A peculiar disease afflicts all kinds of people in America. It attacks executives, professionals and even housewives with equal impunity. The best doctors rarely diagnose it, certainly cannot cure it and, in fact, are often afflicted with it themselves.

It's called information paralysis.

Information paralysis is the inability to proceed from the question to the actual act of beginning to gather information for the answer. Otherwise normal, intelligent people can be made to understand the value of information and even to formulate extremely perceptive questions (see Chapter 3). They can arrive at the most fundamental concept in information consciousness—the realization that they need information. And then—nothing.

Total paralysis strikes. They don't know what to do, where to start, how to go about it. Fear takes over.

The best cure for information paralysis is to become an expert information specialist who is thoroughly familiar with thousands of sources of information. This book is not designed to help you do that. For that matter, we suspect that you do not want to abandon your present career. Instead, we'll try to provide the second-best cure, which involves two things: first, an understanding of the basic types of information sources that exist; and second, an understanding of the basic categories most information needs fall into.

TYPES OF INFORMATION SOURCES

In an earlier chapter we covered the *forms* of information—i.e., primary versus secondary and internal versus external. When you need information— even before you consider any sources—you must first ask yourself what form of information you need. Do you need internal data or information about the external world? Do you need primary or secondary information? (Bear in mind that sources of information can be primary *and* secondary.)

Once you have some idea of the form of information you need, you can start looking. Don't feel paralyzed. There are really only four basic types of sources of information:

(1) Government Sources

(2) Associations

(3) Commercial Publishers, Services and Sources

(4) Libraries

Let's examine each of these in turn.

(1) *Government Sources*

Government sources of information represent a vast depository. The U.S. Government is probably the largest single producer of information, statistics, and facts. It is quite possibly the largest publisher of information. In any case, it is doubtful that anyone collects more information than the Government does through its various branches and agencies.

You must remember that "government" includes local government, state government and federal government, as well as the court systems.

Local government, obviously, is an excellent source of local information. There are in the U.S. over 3,000 counties and over 18,000 cities. County and city clerks keep a wealth of data as do the recorders and registers of deeds. Usually they have information about things like births, deaths, marriages, divorces. They keep property records. They keep information like pet licenses. Most localities have individual departments, like property, tax, building and health. For example, if you were interested in building permit records in a particular locality, you would first go to the Building Department of that locality. Virtually every state also has an association of county commissioners or what is known as an association of counties. These are the groups of county governments within their states.

State governments are also, obviously, excellent sources for statewide information. While each state may be somewhat different, most have a similar array of departments and agencies, such as a secretary of state office that may have many records about companies incorporated in that state; an economic development office that may have information about general economic conditions in the state; a bureau that issues various kinds of licenses such as those for pharmacists or real-estate brokers. Of course, this is just a sample, a limited list. Most states have many other offices that collect information. For example, if you're interested in air pollution in Idaho, you would contact the Bureau of Air Quality, which is part of the Division of Environment, which is, in turn, part of the Idaho Department of Health and Welfare, which happens to be located on the 5th floor of 700 West State Street in Boise. Most states also produce what are known as State Industrial Directories; these are very valuable listings of manufacturing and other companies in the state.

Unlike state and local governments, the Federal Government is not just a source of federal information. It is a source for just about any kind of information imaginable.

The U.S. Government is distinguished by a number of different departments, each with a myriad of individual agencies and bureaus. For example, the Department of Commerce—probably one of the most valuable sources of business information in the world—includes among others, the Bureau of the Census, the Bureau of Economic Analysis, the Economic Development Administration, the Industry and Trade Administration, the Maritime Administration, the National Bureau of Standards, the National Oceanic and Atmospheric Administration, the National Technical Information Service, the Patent and Trademark Office, the Office of Product Standards and the U.S. Travel Service. Each of these divisions of the Department of Commerce has its own information collection and dissemination operation. This pattern is repeated in most of the other government agencies, which range from the Departments of Agriculture, Defense and Energy, to bodies like the Securities & Exchange Commission, the Federal Communications Commission, the Food & Drug Administration and the Interstate Commerce Commission. Many of these agencies, in addition to collecting and disseminating information, also operate full-scale information organizations such as the National Center for Health Statistics, which is part of the Department of Health & Welfare. There is also, by way of example, a U.S. Customs Service Library.

Not to be outdone by the bureaucracy it created, our own U.S. Congress also offers plenty of information sources. Both the Senate and the House have committees and subcommittees (not to mention task forces and project teams) that collect lots of information, much of which gets published in one form or another. For example, if you were interested in obtaining a sample agreement between a franchisor and franchisee, you would find one contained in the records of Congressional hearings on the subject. Access to all this has been made much easier by the existence of a company called the Congressional Information Service, located in Washington, D.C., which publishes an index to the publications of Congress.

One should not forget the Court System either; this includes the Federal and State courts, as well as special courts such as the U.S. Customs Court, the U.S. Tax Court and the U.S. Court of Claims.

In discussing the Government as a source of information—indeed in discussing any network of sources—one should make a distinction between published and unpublished information.

There is a wealth of information collected by the Government that is not published, but is generally available on request, either in writing or by telephone. The Freedom of Information Act was, in part, designed to facilitate the process of requesting information. But much of it has always been available if you tried. Obviously much local and state government information is of limited general interest and merely resides in the appropriate agency—like birth or death records. You must ask for it to get it. The Federal Government publishes more, but also has some rather incredible non-published sources. For example, it has individual experts on virtually every nation in the world, and you can telephone these experts and talk to them!

Published information, of course, emanates from the Federal Government in monumental quantities. There are basic sources like *County Business Patterns* which shows county, state and U.S. statistics on employment, size of reporting business units and payrolls for 15 broad industry categories; and the *Survey of Current Business* which is the official source for the Gross National Product figure; and there are nearly 3000 other statistical series. And then there is Census data, which most people think of as merely population statistics, but which also includes such publications as the *Census of*

Manufacturers; this is a presentation of geographical and industrial data on manufacturers in 500 different industries.

The U.S. Government, in fact, issues so much published material that there is a *Monthly Catalog of United States Government Publications* (available from the Superintendent of Documents, U.S. Government Printing Office). The GPO, as it is called, is probably the single largest "information store" in the world.

(2) *Associations*

Whatever the activity, there seems to be a group that brings together people or organizations involved in that activity. Thus, professional, technical and trade associations, as well as groups like labor unions, are excellent sources of information.

There are probably close to 15,000 such organizations in the U.S., most of which collect information about their activities. Want to know something about frozen food? Try the National Frozen Food Association.

Do you have a sudden interest in beer cans? There's a 12,000-member group called the Beer Can Collectors of America. Do you need information on personnel administration practices? Try the 23,000-member American Society For Personnel Administration. And if it's pet cemeteries you need to know about, yes, there's even an International Association of Pet Cemeteries. It has a whopping 210 members.

Associations are often great starting points when you're looking for information. Frequently, they have a library and publish statistics and other facts on the industries or activities they represent. Furthermore, they can be quite cooperative because, after all, they exist to promote the interests of their members. Of course, it should be kept in mind that their information is not necessarily the most objective.

(3) *Commercial Publishers, Services and Sources*

As suggested in the chapter on the new information environment, there is a vast network of private sector sources that can be tapped, ranging from publishers to information and research services. These can be broken down into a variety of different categories:

(a) *Reference Publications*

There is an absolute multitude of directories, indices, guides, and statistical compilations, not to mention books (like the dictionary), that can be used for informational purposes. Included in this category would be such standard directories as *Standard & Poors Register of Corporations, Directors and Executives* (published by Standard & Poors Corporation, New York City); indices like the *Business Periodicals Index* (published by H.W. Wilson Company, New York City); guides like *Industrial Research Laboratories of the United States* (published by R.R. Bowker Company, New York City) and compilations of statistics like the *Sales & Marketing Management Magazine Survey of Buying Power, (Sales & Marketing Management Magazine*, New York City) which provides a variety of city-by-city data on consumer markets.

There are so many of these publications that we are blessed with such sources of sources as a directory of directories, called *The Guide to American Directories* (published by B. Klein Publications, Coral Springs, Fla.).

(b) *Periodicals*

These days, there is a periodical publication on just about anything, for just about anyone.

For agricultural, chemical and fertilizer producers, there's *Agrichemical Age*. People who make shoes read *Footwear News*. The commercial grape industry on the West Coast is served by *The Good-grape Grower.*

One directory of periodicals lists some 6,000 of them, and most are excellent sources of information, especially those publications that serve specific industries. Want to know something about macaroni? Try the *Macaroni Journal.* No kidding.

What is often missed is that many trade periodicals publish special annual statistical issues or factbooks chock full of the latest annual data about that industry. For example, *Drug Topics* magazine annually publishes its "Red Book" that lists all pharmaceutical products and their wholesale and retail prices. Since magazines tend to be supported by advertising, these annual issues can be very low priced. As another example, *Quick Frozen Foods* magazine publishes a special annual issue that gives statistics on the frozen food industry by product. There are also thousands of newsletters and other serial-type publications.

(c) *Special Information Services*

Depending upon the industry or profession and its information needs, there is a host of special services. For example, the R.L. Polk & Company and Ward's Reports, Inc. both publish a variety of data on the automotive industry. There are loose-leaf services that will keep you updated weekly, monthly or even daily in a field of interest. Organizations like the Conference Board and the Research Institute of America (both in New York City) publish a variety of reports to management on business affairs and other topics. Firms like Arthur D. Little and the Stanford Research Institute produce special reports on industries and markets; these are mailed periodically to members who pay large annual fees and can call upon the firms for consultations. One of the most well-known information services is Dun & Bradstreet, which, along with its many other activities, issues credit reports that are among the few sources of information about privately held companies.

(d) *Information Retrieval Services*

These services will gather just about any information you want for a fee. Please refer to Chapters 7 and 10 for more details.

(e) *Data Bases*

Here again, refer to Chapter 7. It should further be noted that many data bases commercially available on-line are also available in some way in published form as indices or directories. For example, the *F & S Index of Corporations and Industries* (published by Predicasts, Inc., Cleveland, Ohio) is an index that covers company, industry and product information from thousands of periodicals. It was originally available only in published form, but is now also a data base.

(f) *Investigative Services*

This book deals with the subject of information that is available (if you look hard enough) and legally obtained. We're not going to get into industrial espionage or illegal ways of getting information like bribery or wiretapping. But some information is extremely difficult to get. This includes things like background information on individual executives, information on privately held companies, litigation histories, etc. There are a number of investigative services throughout the country that mostly do investigative reports on corporations and executives. Among the better known are companies like Bishop's Services, Inc. If you're about to sign a million-dollar deal with someone you've only known for a few months, it would be the height of folly to rely solely on a cursory check of that person's references. Hire an expert.

(g) *Market Research & Survey Firms*

These are mostly firms engaged in primary research activities of one sort or another—i.e., they are out there talking directly to individual people to find things out. Or they are directly measuring, through survey methods, things like sales of products. Four different types of these are commonly identified:

First are firms that run what are called consumer panels. These are carefully put together and established groups of individual consumers who periodically report on various aspects of their buying behavior, attitudes and intentions, using diaries or other techniques. Typical of the firms that run consumer panels are National Family Opinion, Inc. and Market Research Corporation of America. These consumer panels are highly useful when you want, for example, to have a continual measurement of consumer attitudes toward your product.

A second type of firm conducts what are called store or warehouse audits on either a syndicated or customized basis. In syndicated audits, firms like A.C. Nielsen and Selling Areas Marketing, Inc. (a Time, Inc. division known as SAMI) continuously monitor the movement of products through stores by type of product and brand and even package size; they compile the results and sell them for very high prices.

A third type of firm in this area is the firm that collects information from extensive field interviews and then compiles and publishes that information. A typical one would be the F.W. Dodge Division of McGraw-Hill Information Systems; this company collects building construction data through hundreds of interviewers. It supplements this with other information and publishes thousands of reports each month on building projects.

A fourth type of firm is one that conducts actual consumer surveys on either a syndicated or custom basis. Typical of syndicated surveys is the regularly issued Gallup poll where results are offered to many participants. Some firms run what are called "omnibus" surveys which regularly survey a national probability sample of respondents. Custom surveys, of course, can be done on just about any subject. About 1,500 is the right number of people from whom to obtain a nationally representative sample, in most cases.

(4) *Libraries*

The fourth basic source is libraries. There are many types of libraries, including public, university, college and what are called "special libraries." It is these latter ones that are actually the most interesting—they are the special, private libraries located in businesses and other institutions. While not public, many of them will in fact make their information available to you. Some of the special libraries are the only source for information you may need. For example, if you wanted to know something about the college life of an alumnus of Yale, you would have to find someone who went there and have him go to the library in the Yale Club of New York City to consult the old yearbooks.

Many of the large public libraries are right on top of the latest developments in the information environment and even have access to data bases—and will perform data-base searching.

Although this is not a source book on information, what we have just done is to quickly review the major *types* of information sources. We have done this to give you ideas on starting points so that you aren't afflicted with information paralysis. Whatever your question, an answer can most likely be found within information stored or disseminated by some government body, some association or group, a library or a commercial publisher or service.

But which government body? Which service?

That's where the source books come in handy (See Appendices). But, there's quick help available, if you don't want to read a source book. And that's to consult sources of sources. There are a very few of these that are of such all-encompassing value that we can list them here, in response to the key questions you might have.

What Federal Government body or agency can help me?

Source: Researcher's Guide to Washington
Washington Researchers
918 16th Street, NW
Washington, DC 20006

Is there an association that can help?

Source: The Encyclopedia of Associations
Gale Research Company
Book Tower
Detroit, MI 48226

Is there an information service that can help me?

Sources: Encyclopedia of Information Systems and Services
Gale Research Co.
Book Tower
Detroit, MI 48226

Information Sources
The Membership Directory of the Information Industry
   Association
316 Pennsylvania Ave., SE
Washington, DC

The Directory of Fee-Based Information Services
Information Alternative
P.O. Box 657
Woodstock, NY 12498

Is there a data base that can answer my question?

Sources: Computer-Readable Data Bases
(A Directory and Data Sourcebook)
American Society for Information Science
1155 16th Street, NW
Washington, DC 20036

Directory of Online Databases
Cuadra Associates. Inc.
1523 Sixth Street, Suite 12
Santa Monica, CA 90401

The Computer Bank Book
(The Executive Guide to Computer Data Banks)
FIND/SVP
500 Fifth Avenue
New York, NY 10036

Information Market Place
R.R. Bowker Company
1180 Avenue of the Americas
New York, NY 10036

Is there a periodical on this subject?

Sources: The Standard Periodical Directory
Oxbridge Communications, Inc.
183 Madison Avenue
New York, NY 10016

Ulrich's International Periodicals Directory
R.R. Bowker Company
1180 Avenue of the Americas
New York, NY 10036

Is there a market research firm or published study that can help me?

Sources: International Directory of Marketing Research Houses and
Services
New York Chapter, Inc.
American Marketing Association
420 Lexington Avenue
New York, NY 10017

FINDEX: The Directory of Market Research Reports,
Studies and Surveys
FIND/SVP
500 Fifth Avenue
New York, NY 10036

Is there a library that can help me?

Sources: Directory of Special Libraries and Information Centers
Gale Research Company
Book Tower
Detroit, MI 48226

American Library Directory
R.R. Bowker Company
1180 Avenue of the Americas
New York, NY 10036

CATEGORIES OF INFORMATION

The second part of our cure for information paralysis is to gain an understanding of the different categories of external information.

If you are in business or in the professions, there are certain categories of information that you are likely to need. Indeed, it is inconceivable that you can exist properly without them. These are as follows:

(1) First of all, you need information about your competition—about other companies, organizations or individuals. This means

you must have information both about individual competitors and about your industry or profession.

(2) You need information about your market, whether that market consists of individual consumers or other organizations and companies.

(3) You need information about the world that surrounds you insofar as it may affect your business or profession. This means you need information on the environment, politics, economics, culture and government.

(4) You need information on the best way to do business. This means you need information on how to manage, how to organize, how to run your business.

(5) You need information on scientific and technological developments. If you're not "up" on the latest, you could be down and out shortly.

(6) Finally, you need information on laws, regulations and other restrictions that may affect the way you do business.

If you can start thinking in terms of categories, you can begin to break down your information needs so that you can properly direct yourself to the right types of sources which we described earlier.

COMPETITION

Surely, in a country as populated as ours, you have competition in whatever field you are in. And most assuredly your success will depend, to some degree, on the amount and quality of information you can glean about your competitor(s). Whether you are a consultant, or you are running a small hair salon, or you are the president of a multinational corporation, information about your competition is *not* an elective. Yet the number of people who ignore this kind of scrutiny is astounding.

(Once again, please understand that the subject of industrial espionage is irrelevant to what is being discussed here.)

Another thing. Multitudes of executives lose their jobs and professional people lose clients daily. Why is this so? Undoubtedly because they are not performing their functions adequately. One of the keys to performance is information about your competition. If you are not worried about your competition, chances are that you will lose your job; and if you are self-employed, you will probably lose your business.

What kind of information should you have about your competition? Here's a rudimentary check-list:

— their management structure
— product lines
— sales
— financial condition
— facilities
— any information on new products, new directions they are taking
— marketing approaches

Is this kind of information available? In all likelihood, much of it is. The means to obtain it vary.

One approach is by word of mouth. A funny story points this up. Dave and Sam were partners in the ladies' garment business for many years. During one season, they had incredibly bad luck. When they produced satins, organdies were the rage. When they produced nylon, cotton came into vogue, etc. One day Dave came to work so depressed that he bid Sam good-bye and jumped out of their 36th-story window. Sam ran to the open window, appalled. As Dave hurtled past the fourteenth floor, he glanced into the window of a competitor and yelled up to his partner, "Sam, they're cutting velvets in there!" This would come under the heading of competing "new products in development." One approach—not too accurate, and a bit extreme.

Word of mouth, however, is not always possible. But if you start thinking about the different types of sources we described earlier, you can quickly begin to get a grasp of how to proceed.

For example, if your competitor is a publicly held corporation, then it must file information with the government. If that is so, then there must be an agency within the government that compiles or makes available such information. Of course, there is. It's the Securities & Exchange Commission.

If your competitor is a privately held corporation, then it is likely that information will be much harder to find. And it is. But there are services like Dun & Bradstreet that will provide credit reports; there are published indices that might index anything that has been written about the company; there are local Chambers of Commerce that might keep data on how the company does business; there are investigative services that will look into the background of the principals, etc.

Similarly, if you want to keep tabs on the state of your industry, each of the types of sources we covered earlier probably has one or more items of data that can help you put together a complete picture.

But the primary reason for the necessity and urgency of gathering information about your competition has undoubtedly occurred to you by now. *All of the above information-gathering methods are available to your competition as well!* You are undoubtedly being studied by a competitor at this very moment.

MARKETS

Everyone needs information on their markets. If you sell your product or service to individual consumers, then you are likely to need information about their habits, their buying patterns, their feelings and intentions. As such, you would direct yourself toward the market research firms and survey firms that specialize in such things. Or you may want information about the products and services—competitive or related—that such consumers buy. In this case you may direct yourself to syndicated audits we mentioned that measure the movement of goods through retail outlets.

If you sell your product or service to businesses or organizations, then in order to obtain information about your market you'll have to get information about the industries you serve. You would direct yourself, therefore, to associations and trade periodicals that serve the industries. You might explore what the government knows about those industries.

Here's a tip on getting information about markets. When you need a quick look at the size of a market, try catalogues of mailing-list firms. They are virtually free and make for fascinating reading, not to mention the fact that they contain tremendous stores of marketing information. For example, let's assume you've just invented a revolutionary rack for holding and displaying automobile tires. You figure it would sell like hotcakes to tire retailers and auto supply stores. But how many of them are there? Well, a glance at the mailing lists available from a firm like Ed Burnett Consultants, Inc. (NYC) shows it has a list of 42,300 tire and tube retailers and 102,950 auto supply and accessory retailers. Of course, their lists may not include *all* your potential market. But they do include a very, very important part of it—the part that can be reached by mail!

Another thing to keep in mind is that, generally speaking, the narrower the market, the more unlikely it is that data has been collected in a readily available format. Conversely, the broader the market, the more available the data. Cosmetics would be a broad market; green eye shadow would be a narrow one. It is extremely easy to find published, available studies that have already been done on the cosmetics industry and market. We know of no complete study on green eye shadow, however.

THE WORLD

Every day, every section of your local newspaper has something in it which directly or indirectly affects your business or profession—including the advertisements. The newspaper may not give you a totally realistic picture of what the world is like (you must rely on your intellect for that), but it does give you an accurate picture of how your community is perceiving that world and, therefore, how its attitudes and values are being shaped and formed. You need this knowledge desperately for your own success in your business.

Moving further outward . . . national and international magazines and newspapers . . . give us both in-depth information and a wider perspective. If your business is to grow, you cannot afford to be either xenophobic or provincial in your outlook.

All types of sources have information about various aspects of the world around us. The problem is that most often we need more information about the world than we realize and there are more sources than we can imagine.

Let's go back to the example on Brazil in the data-base section of this book. Assume that you make the deal with the guy in Brazil and you are now an exporter to that country. What's happening there is of paramount importance to you. So, too, what's happening in South America in general is germane. You might now consult the New York Times Information Bank every month for updates on what's been written about Brazil. You'll want to consult the country expert on Brazil in the Federal Government. You'll suddenly want to know whether there are any private information services that can help, and you'll discover a company called Business International, Inc. (New York City) that specializes in collecting and disseminating information on business activity and economic developments in foreign countries.

MANAGEMENT PRACTICE

We have a tendency to do things without pondering whether we are doing them right or wrong, whether there is a better way, or how others are doing the same things.

Suppose an executive wants to start a pension plan for his employees. Usually his first impulse is to call in a pension expert. But he should think first about reading something on the subject. Why doesn't he? Laziness? Not necessarily. The answer comes back again to the lack of information consciousness. It is always fine to call in experts, but surely the executive himself should be *prepared* for that meeting.

Let's take another example. Suppose you wish to hire a data-processing person. Yours is a small company which is growing quickly. You bought a computer and you need someone to run it. How much must you pay for a competent data-processing person? Most people call a personnel agency and inquire. But the agency's answer is necessarily biased, isn't it? An information-conscious person would immediately realize that there must be a salary survey of data processors available by region and that he could buy that survey.

So, too, with expenditure norms like advertising, rent, payroll, etc. Some folks are afraid to inquire for fear of discovering that they have been managing their businesses or professions poorly for a very long time. But those people lack curiosity and have either discarded this book chapters ago, or never purchased it at all.

Our country publishes 37,000 new book titles each year. But with a population of 220,000,000 it only takes less than 100,000 copies sold for a title to hit the bestseller list. So much for literary curiosity. And did you know that the books which hold answers to your questions can be found in *The Subject Guide To Books In Print*? (R.R. Bowker, New York City.)

GOVERNMENT REGULATIONS

Government regulations on any level—town, county, state or federal—are such an integral (albeit horrendous) part of everyone's business or professional life that ignorance of this informational area can lead to total failure and destruction. Regulations are a vital part of your external environment.

If, for example, you want to manufacture a new detergent and you don't know that county regulations would automatically ban its production because of one of its chemical ingredients, you are courting disaster.

The only saving grace about this kind of information is that governments distribute published regulations free of charge on request. Your tax dollars pay for this dissemination. What is required of you is your time to locate and send for it.

You now have the prescription for curing whatever degree of information paralysis you may be suffering from. But, like all prescriptions, two more steps are required: you must fill it and then use it. The types and sources of information are all there on the "medicinal" shelves. You have only to reach for them according to your particular needs—and there is no way that you can "overdose."

CHAPTER 9

Putting It All Into Practice

So far, we've told you how to ask questions. We've discussed the cost and value of information. We've shown you a new information environment. We've cured (hopefully) any lingering information paralysis. You're beginning to think like an information-conscious person. But, if you're like most people, you want a test run. You want to see how it's all put together in practice.

Since everyone's information needs are different, this is difficult. But we'll try. We'll take a very common information problem—the need for information on a particular industry—and go through all the steps required to solve it.

Assume you developed a new type of widget. You need information on the widget industry. Assume further that you need to present this information in the form of a report.

The very first thing you would do would be to find out whether anyone else has done a study on the widget industry or any aspect of it. This would save you the trouble of researching and writing your own report. If not, you would then proceed to put one together yourself by gathering all the information.

Typically, your report should include:

(1) a description of the widget industry

(2) a description and analysis of the market for widgets

(3) the supplier industry structure—i.e. how the industry is organized

(4) a description of the end-users or consumers

(5) factors affecting the industry/market

Section by section, here's what your report should cover, with an indication of the information to include and the questions you should be asking yourself along the way:

(1) *The Industry*

Possible sub-sections: Introduction, History and Background, Products, Equipment, Technology, Product Applications, Trends in the Industry, History of New Product Introductions.

This section's main purpose is to answer a very simple question: "What industry are we talking about here?"

In most cases, this section will cover the following:

— Definition of the industry. What is the widget business?

— History of the industry: How did it develop? Where and when did it start?

— What products and/or product groups make up the industry?

— Product descriptions

(Many reports fail to describe adequately the products being covered. Descriptions should include technical details.)

— What are the products used for? (Product applications)

— How are the products made? Any special processes or equipment?

— Impact of technological developments.

— Anything special/unusual about this industry that is a key to understanding it? Examples: patent expirations, profit margins, tax or tariff policies and government regulations.

Depending upon the industry, some of the items above may require full sub-sections within this section. In the case of highly technical products or in the case of high-technology industries, a discussion of technology might even be contained within another *main* section of the report.

(2) *The Market*

Possible sub-sections: Introduction, The Size of the Market, The Market by Product Type, The Market by End-Use Sector, Sales by Outlet, Future Trends.

This section should cover the following:

— The size of the overall market in dollars and in units

— Dollar and unit sales by product category or type

— Dollar and unit sales by end-use sector

— Dollar and unit sales by outlet

— Imports and exports

— Sales by region or geographic area (especially if sales are regional in nature)

In each case, figures should be given for the past five years and projections should be given for next year, three years from now, and five years from now. Past actual and future projected annual growth rates should be given, with comment on the effects of inflation.

Let's take an ideal example: Assume the widget industry consists of steel, aluminum and plastic widgets. Each of the three types is made either by a wet or dry process and sold through retailers, mass merchandisers and auto supply stores. Major users are a few individuals, but mostly local governments and company fleets. A good market study will show, then, the size (in units and dollars) of the overall widget industry and the breakdown by steel, aluminum, and plastic. A table will show sales of widgets by wet and dry process, broken down by steel, aluminum, and plastic, if possible. The percentage of sales of each type by outlet (retailers, mass merchandisers and auto supply) will be given as will the percentage of each type sold by the end-use market.

Of course, not all markets are ideal, but a good study will strive for maximum breakdown and segmentation.

Figures in dollars should always be identified. Are they dollars at the manufacturers' level, wholesale level, or the retail level? Are they constant dollars?

The depth to which this section will go is also dependent on the size, type and scope of your needs. If they are limited, your budget will also be. So your study will obviously have to rely on published data which is sometimes good and sometimes poor. In very narrow markets, estimates frequently have to be developed.

If estimates have to be developed for most of the market size tables, it is rare that such estimates can be done for past years, so it is better to concentrate on figures for the current year and for future years.

Studies performed very early or very late in a year should include estimates for that year. For example, a study done in late 1977 or early 1978 will usually include reliable figures for 1976, but figures may not yet be available for 1977. The study should make sure estimates for 1977 are included as well as projections for 1978.

This section should make ample use of charts and tables, and the text should summarize the key points in the tables as well as discuss trends and growth rates.

The success of your report will almost always hinge on how well organized and complete this section is. This is especially true for studies requiring estimates due to the lack of secondary data.

There are pitfalls to be aware of. Some examples:

— domestic consumption of a product is usually thought of as manufacturers' shipments plus imports less exports. This may not be true in industries where retailers or wholesalers keep very large inventories or when an impending strike causes an inventory build-up.

— when the market consists largely of imports it is vital to understand how much the value of the landed import (including duty) is marked up by the importer before he sells it to a wholesaler/distributor or retailer.

— secondary sources are often inaccurate or confusing in identifying the size of the market in terms of manufacturers' or retail dollars. One source consistently identifies its figures for certain industries as being "factory shipments" or factory level dollars, but close examination reveals that imports are included.

— the definition of product categories in one source may differ from another. For example, if the U.S. Government had import figures for "widgets," the particular widgets included might be different from those included in a magazine's figures for sales of widgets.

(3) *Supplier Industry Structure*

Possible sub-sections: Introduction, Competition or Companies in the Field, Pricing, Margins and Mark-Ups, Distribution Methods, Advertising and Promotion, Company Profiles.

Once the size of the market has been covered, and you know how much of each product is sold through what outlets and to whom, the next step is to describe the suppliers/manufacturers of the products. Who are they, where do they stand in relation to one another, and how do they bring their products to the marketplace?

The most important part of this section is to identify the leading companies in the field and their respective share of market. Some historical perspective on their market-share position should also be provided.

The competitive situation can usually be covered in one of two ways. In the less expensive studies, or in industries dominated by just a few companies, the general description of each company and the market share data can usually be covered in one section of the report. In more in-depth studies or those covering industries with many major companies, it is often necessary to augment such a section with a separate section called "Company Profiles" in which each company is described in detail.

If there is no company profile section, then the section on the competition should at least include:

— identification of major and secondary companies in the field,

— their sales of the product(s) covered in dollars and, if possible, in units,

— their current market-share position and historical trend,

— major differences between the companies in terms of management, manufacturing processes, marketing methods, etc.,

— major differences in product lines, product types, etc.,

— major competitive trends.

If a company profile section is included, it is usually then possible to go into further details on each company. Such details may include:

— names of top management

— complete description of product(s) within the industry being covered by this report

— dollar sales of company as a whole and for products or product line being covered in this study; profitability

— important parent/subsidiary relationships

— manufacturing facilities; methods, cost factors; availability of resources; labor contracts

— company organization and structure; marketing philosophy and practice; franchises; international operations

— new products; research and development expenditures; technological advantages or disadvantages

Structuring the market study with or without company profiles often presents a problem. If there are no profiles, the section describing the competitive situation and different companies in the industry can get bogged down in details on each company. If there are profiles, inserting them immediately after a summary competitive section with market shares can interrupt the flow of the study. Thus, if company profiles are included, it is often wise to include them as an Appendix or as a separate section at the end of the report but prior to the appendices.

Some in-depth reports (especially those done for acquisition purposes) may require even greater depth of information about some or all of the major companies in the field. Such information might include actual operating financial figures, organization charts, locations of plants, biographies of key principals, a bibliography of articles about each company, clippings of advertising placed by the company, copies of annual reports or 10-K's, etc. Generally, all of these should be included as appendices, and not written into the main body of the study.

Of course, the depth of information required on each major and/or minor company will depend mostly on the depth and cost of the study as a whole.

Whatever the budget, however, a frequent error in many studies is the failure to include at least a list of the major and secondary companies in the field with their *exactly* correct names and addresses and the *brand names* of the products they have in the industry covered by the study. For example: Assume a leading product in the widget industry is called Widgetco and that it is distributed in the U.S. by a company called the American Widget Company. Assume the American Widget Company only assembles Widgetco and that the parts are actually made in Germany by the International Widget Company which happens to own 80% of the American Widget Company, located in Dallas. All of this information should be made abundantly clear in the study, and the list of producers should include both the American Widget Company and its parent, the International Widget Company.

The section on the Supplier Industry Structure should also cover pricing, distribution methods and advertising and promotion. Usually, these will be three different sub-sections, but that will depend on the individual study.

The sub-section on pricing should give you an idea of price ranges of the various product categories. Such a section can also include one of the key areas of a good market study—a detailed discussion of margins and mark-ups. What is the manufacturers' margin? How much are the products marked up at each level in the distribution process?

The sub-section on distribution should provide a complete description of the methods of distribution used in the industry, including any differences between the methods of the industry leaders. Here's a list of typical items to be covered:

— description of manufacturers' sales organization
  are the products sold by manufacturers' salesmen? if so, how? how many salesmen? how are territories divided?

— role of warehouses, if any

— role of wholesalers/jobbers/manufacturers reps/agents/importers
  is the distribution accomplished mainly through any of these? if so, how? which major manufacturers use which? what are payment terms, commission rates, mark-ups? how much control do manufacturers have over reps? training of reps and agents?

— role of retailers
  what are the major types of retail outlets used? role of mass merchandisers; catalog showrooms? geographical distribution?

retailer's expected turnover on yearly basis? what is retail mark-up; margin? what are payment terms? any discounts? price cutting? any coop advertising allowances? merchandising?

A very extensive in-depth study might include as appendices a table of all products and recent retail prices; a map showing geographical distribution of warehouses, retail outlets and wholesalers; charts showing sales or distribution organizations; specific documents showing agreements between manufacturers and distributors, etc.

The sub-section on advertising and promotion should tell you how the industry talks to its end-users. What advertising media are being used, how much is being spent overall and by whom, and what are the sales messages being conveyed? Appendix support for this section might include details of advertising expenditures by company for the past several years, tear sheets of actual ads, transcripts of TV or radio ads, packaging types, list of industry periodicals and trade shows, etc.

(4) *End-Users (or) Consumers*

Possible sub-sections: Introduction, Market Potential and Penetration, The Typical End-User, Consumer Demographics, Consumer Surveys.

The exact title and organization of this section of your report depends, obviously, on whether your widgets are sold to businesses or consumers or both.

While many studies offer a good assessment of the present size of the market in terms of dollar and unit sales of the products, few studies really discuss the *potential* size of the market and the current penetration. For example, it is valuable to know how many widgets are being sold this year, but it is also valuable to know how many potential users of widgets there are in the marketplace and how many widgets are actually out there in use.

This section should then go on to cover the following:

— Who buys the product(s) covered in this study?

If businesses, what kind of businesses? Who is the key individual buyer? If consumers, what are the demographics, characteristics?

— Why is the product purchased or not purchased?

What are the economic factors involved? (Disposable income, inflation, recession, etc.) Psychological factors (who makes purchasing decision?)

Product factors which differentiate the products (price, size, delivery, accessories, warranties, advertising, etc.)

— Where and how do end-users buy the product(s)?

— Any trends in end-users/consumers?

In many cases the results of published surveys of end-users/consumers are available, and these should obviously be summarized within the text of the report. If an end-user survey was performed in connection with the market study, then its results would be very prominently featured and discussed.

Demographic profiles of consumers (especially for products sold in supermarkets) are frequently available.

(5) *Factors Affecting The Industry/Market*

Possible sub-sections: Government Regulations, World Conditions, New Technology, Strikes, Embargoes.

This section should be used to cover any factors which influence the industry or market. In most cases, government regulations (their description and impact) will be the major factor discussed.

GETTING THE INFORMATION FOR THE STUDY

Once you've outlined the information needed, you now have to go out and find it.

The easiest thing to do is to hire an information retrieval service or other information supplier to do it for you. But if you'd rather do it yourself, here's a checklist—by no means all-inclusive—of steps to take:

(Many of these steps can be applied to virtually any information need.)

(1) As previously mentioned, find out whether anyone has already done a study on the subject. If someone has, and it contains the information you need, you've saved yourself a lot of money.

(2) Perform a five-year retrospective search of published literature (articles, etc.) on widgets, using both computer data bases and manual methods. Then, retrieve the full text of all apparently relevant articles you find referenced or summarized in the data bases and indices. Depending on the industry, keep in mind that major overview articles about an industry are occasionally missed if they have appeared in publications that are not indexed or not well indexed.

(3) Contact the widget industry association, if there is one, and have them send you whatever information may be relevant. If there is no association, explore to see whether there may be associations in related fields.

(4) Obtain data on advertising expenditures by companies making widgets. There are commercial information services that do this. (Example: Leading National Advertisers, Inc., in New York City.) The reason this is important is that it will help identify those

companies that are actively advertising their widgets and how much they spend on advertising; this can help define the size of their operations.

(5) If your widgets are going to be sold to consumers, you should immediately obtain whatever information may be available from audit firms like A.C. Nielsen and SAMI. Note that this data will be expensive, but it's worth it.

(6) Make sure you get technical specifications and product descriptions, as well as product catalogues, on competitive widget products. Any patent information can be obtained from the U.S. Government. Catalogues are very useful information sources and can often be obtained simply by calling the individual companies. There is also a variety of commercial information services that have product information.

(7) Check Wall Street investment firms to see if they've written reports on either the widget industry or individual companies in the industry. These reports, written for investment advisory purposes, often contain much valuable research information. Note: many of these firms no longer give these reports away free, but they are generally available from the firms themselves or from distributors like FIND/SVP or Frost & Sullivan (both in New York City) at prices under $500.

(8) Get data on imports and exports of widgets from the Department of Commerce.

(9) Get all relevant data on the widget industry from the Census of Manufacturers and other U.S. Government publications.

(10) Get any data on widgets from such sources as Standard & Poors Industry Surveys, annual issues of periodicals, and any other guides and directories. Don't forget to check whether any books have been written on widgets; refer to *Books In Print* (R.R. Bowker, N.Y.C.)

(11) Order tear sheets of advertisements on widgets. There are services like Packaged Facts in New York City, that will do this for you. You can also obtain copies of television and radio commercials if necessary.

(12) From all of the foregoing, plus any industry directories or general directories like Thomas' Register of American Manufacturers, make a list of all companies in the industry and begin gathering company data as follows:

— annual report, if available. call the company to get it

— copies of all Securities & Exchange Commission filings, if the company is public

— product catalogues

— parent/subsidiary relationships

— retrospective search of the published literature on the major companies in the field

— Dun & Bradstreet reports on the privately held companies

— use services or data bases like Economic Information Systems to obtain any available market share information on individual companies or manufacturing plants

While this is by no means an exhaustive list of secondary research techniques that can be used, it does cover most of the basic steps essential to getting information on the widget industry. Once you have gathered all the foregoing, you should have a pretty good picture of the widget business.

Then, you're ready for primary research; i.e. interviews with industry sources, companies, end-users, etc.

From the information gathered it is usually possible to identify a number of possible experts on the industry. These can be authors of major articles about the industry in the trade press, or they can be individuals in associations, or those who are quoted frequently in the articles you have gathered. These people can usually be called on the telephone and interviewed about trends and developments that have not yet been reported.

Then you should certainly conduct telephone and—where possible—in-person interviews with manufacturers, wholesalers, distributors and retailers of widgets.

Finally, you can commission an independent, objective custom survey of consumers or end-users of widgets to ask them just about anything you feel you may need to know—ranging from how many widgets they buy each year to what color widget they prefer.

How much will all this cost? How long will it take?

It varies, of course, on the type of industry and market being examined. If done by an outside firm for you, you can figure that a complete, thorough examination of an industry should require at least two months' time and will cost between $10,000 and $30,000, not counting a survey of consumers or end-users. Such a survey might add anywhere from $10,000 to $50,000 to the cost, depending on the size of the respondent sample surveyed, the number of questions asked, the tabulations required, etc.

By way of comparison, if you elected to do the exact same report completely by yourself, it could probably take you about two or three times as long, not counting the survey of consumers or end-users. Thus, if you earn $40,000 a year and it takes you six months, the cost would be $20,000 of your time. Of course, this doesn't include the opportunity cost (the money you have lost by spending six months researching).

CHAPTER 10

Organizing Your Information-Gathering System

We stated at the beginning of this book that most people have little idea about how to find out what they need to know. Given this, it is not surprising that most people—and the organizations they work in—do not have an effective information-gathering system. How to create one is the subject of this chapter.

Effective information-gathering systems begin, at the simplest level, with the individual—with you.

Let's say you're the operator of a retail establishment. You, or your surrogate, "shop" your nearest competitor once every six months to determine his prices and stock. You remind yourself to do this on your calendar. You have started a regular six-month watch; you have installed a system.

Information gathering, in other words, begins with the individual. Whether you are a single shopkeeper, owner of a small business, consultant, or executive in a large corporation, you must be organized to benefit from information that will further your personal position. You need to be personally aware of your competition. You need the most current journals, books, directories and other periodicals in your field. You need to make sure you are up to date.

This may seem painfully obvious, yet it is amazing to see how many otherwise sensible people fail to systematically keep themselves informed within their own field of interest. For example, it is estimated that there are 100,000 consultants in the U.S. Yet only about 20,000 subscribe to the trade periodicals in their individual fields.

As a simple checklist, ask yourself these questions:

— Do I belong to the principal trade or professional organizations in my field? Do I take the time to actually read them?

— Do I subscribe to the principal trade or professional magazines in my field. Do I take the time to actually read them?

— Do I periodically take the time to check up on key competitors, products, trends, government regulations or other factors that may affect me personally?

— Do I at least occasionally glance through my junk mail? (It's amazing what one can learn from this!)

— Am I familiar with my internal information resources (my shelf of books; my company library)? Do I have a list of outside information/research suppliers I can call on when necessary?

If you can't answer yes to all the above questions, you have an inadequate personal information-gathering system. As a result, you probably have inadequate knowledge. Relying on friends, contacts, accountants, lawyers and advisors is highly useful, but it is not a substitute for a system.

Moving up from the individual to the organization, the information-gathering function becomes a more complex issue, and the system will depend to a great extent on the size of your organization. The steps in creating that system, however, are the same.

The first step is to decide under whose direction the principal information-gathering function will be. In very small companies or proprietorships, it is usually the president or should be. In larger companies, information gathering generally falls within the marketing, planning, or R&D function, but is often fragmented in many different areas.

It is important to remember that information-gathering and research functions can be organized by product lines, by customer groups, by sales regions or by corporate functions. For example, Product A and Product B may each have their own market research departments. Or there may be an information system for industrial, consumer and government markets. Or each regional office of a company may have its own information set-up. In other organizations, the information and research operation is centralized and serves all operating departments, regardless of product, market or area.

All too often, the information function is buried in "administration" somewhere, frequently as an adjunct of the data-processing department. This arises because of a confusion between internal and external information. A data-processing department is concerned with keeping track of a company's internal data and should not be responsible for gathering external information. These are two entirely different activities.

This will change somewhat as technologies converge and companies develop top-level information executives with overall responsibility for all the information resources of an organization, both internal and external. But unless and until your organization has such an "Information Manager" the gathering of external information should be a function within the departments of those people who need external information the most; i.e., marketing, sales, research, planning or top management.

Once you have decided who should be responsible for the organization of the information-gathering function, the next step is to establish a library or information center.

In the smaller organizations, the "library" may be nothing more than a shelfful or roomful of reference materials. These may include industry handbooks, catalogs, trade magazines, directories that cover your field, annual reports of your customers, suppliers, competitors. Typically, the small library should have such basic information sources as Thomas' Register, the U.S. Statistical Abstract, Business Periodicals Index, Encyclopedia of Associations, Predicasts' F&S Index, Dun & Bradstreet Million and Middle Market Directories, plus statistical issues of appropriate trade publications. One suggestion, if your mini-library will not have a full-time librarian, put a manager in charge of maintaining it. Don't expect busy secretaries to do it. This is especially true if you intend to have a terminal to access available data bases, as mentioned in Chapter 7.

The next step up is to create your own *staffed* internal library/information center. It may be small or big and may service anything from a law office to a large industrial complex. Such a library must be staffed by a professional librarian or information manager. This is the individual you will call upon for any and all external information. This is the person who will know how to collect information, how to disseminate it, how to keep records.

Of course, you should have sufficient information needs to warrant the expense of your own information center. Staffed by one professional and one assistant or clerical person such an information center can easily cost $75,000 a year, not including overhead. How can you tell when you need one? You probably do if your company is buying endless duplicate copies of books and magazines, if reference materials are piling up all over, if substantial money is being spent calling all around the U.S. in search of statistics, if research being done is less than thorough, if decisions are being delayed because of lack of information. You definitely need one if your employees are leaving to go to companies with better information resources.

If you do decide to establish an information center, make sure top management is involved in its creation. Set up goals, budgets, space requirements, etc. Hire a fully qualified individual. If you don't know how to go about this, contact a consultant or the Special Libraries Association in New York City. Make sure the individuals involved are familiar with computer data bases and their possibilities. You want a library that will lead you forward into the 21st Century, not backward into the 19th.

Unfortunately, the vast majority of organizations are simply too small to be able to afford even a small in-house library. Even companies with information centers often find their resources too limited or their staffs overburdened. Further, with the amount of available information increasing, the time required to find what you need is becoming more and more costly. So whether large or small, with libraries or without, many organizations are looking for information assistance.

Enter the information retrieval service.

Information retrieval services are organizations that gather information on request for a fee. Also frequently referred to as information brokers, information retailers and information-on-demand companies, these services began to emerge in the 1970's, not-so-coincidentally with the emergence of computer data banks. As we saw in Chapter 7, retailers commonly perform data-base searches. But a good information retrieval service can do far more. A top-notch retrieval service can generally offer the following capabilities:

(1) Access to readily available information in its own extensive, up-to-date library. The larger retrieval services maintain information centers containing far more reference materials than most companies could afford to purchase by themselves.

(2) Access to a staff of highly trained and experienced information specialists—researchers who have the expertise to track down the information you need in a rapid, cost-effective way.

(3) Access to a wide variety of computer data bases, so it can perform searches on request.

(4) The knowledge and ability necessary to translate your questions and problems into realistic information-gathering steps.

(5) The ability to perform in-depth market studies, surveys, field interviews and other research activities, including monitoring and current-awareness services.

(6) The ability to retrieve copies of articles, government documents, annual reports, catalogues, product samples, or whatever else you might need.

(7) The expertise necessary to assist you in developing—and even maintaining—your own internal library in conjunction with cost-effective use of outside services.

There are large information retrieval firms offering many services, and there are small outfits consisting of individual freelance researchers. The actual extent of services offered usually varies with the size of the retailer. (A selected list of these services is in the appendix.)

A point to remember about these information retrieval services is that they mostly supply just the facts—not the analysis. As such they differ from consulting firms or traditional survey research firms. Of course, they are also significantly less costly than consultants, and many do offer a creative, consultative approach to information gathering.

The advantage of using an information retrieval service is that all you have to do is ask the question. They take it from there. But fair warning: when you call such a service, try to make sure that you and they understand clearly what the question is, how extensive a search you need, when you need the results and in what form.

As previously stated, most information retrieval services charge between $20 and $75 per hour. Some work on a project basis; others on an hourly basis. Some have retainer agreements under which they act as your ongoing information center, responding to your daily or weekly reference needs in addition to larger assignments.

We've tried to describe various possibilites for organizing an information-gathering function. How should you organize yours? It obviously depends upon your requirements, but here are some general guidelines:

If your organization is small, and your needs for information are infrequent, you should rely mostly on information retrieval services.

If you are small, but have frequent needs, you may want to have a small internal library plus access to one or more computer data bases that will be used frequently. This can be supplemented by access to outside suppliers such as retrieval services, market research firms, consultants and the like.

If yours is a large firm with infrequent needs, you should initially imitate the small, infrequent user. But something may be wrong, because a large organization should need information regularly. Examine and evaluate how information is obtained by your people. Most large firms really should have at least a small library, if only to centralize needlessly duplicated copies of subscriptions.

If you are a large, frequent user, you should have your own, fully staffed information center whose activities may be supplemented by a wide variety of outside services. Some of these services may be purchased through the information center itself; others by individual executives. In the latter case, it is usually wise to centralize basic facts about the outside services within the library. In this manner you can avoid using services that may have performed badly for others within your firm.

Conclusion

The return on an investment in information is knowledge.

At what level is your information consciousness now? Hopefully much higher than when you started this book. If not, the reasons can only be the following:

(1) You had a very high level of information consciousness when you started.

(2) You are an information specialist who bought this book out of curiosity.

(3) You have not paid attention.

(4) You have paid attention, but we have not been able to communicate with you—in which case, you deserve a full refund.

Assuming, however, that we have succeeded, your first step should be to attempt to raise the information-consciousness level of anyone who works with you; colleague, secretary or associate. The second step is to quickly calculate all the time you will save, and translate that into money and effort. Put this money and this effort into new ventures. The third step is to observe how quickly the light turns green for you at every juncture because of your constant state of preparation.

About
the Authors

Andrew P. Garvin is chairman and chief executive officer of FIND/SVP, The Information Clearinghouse, a leading information retrieval service. He is a member of the Board of Directors of the Information Industry Association and was chairman of the 1979 National Information Conference and Exposition.

Co-founded by Mr. Garvin in 1970, FIND/SVP is part of the worldwide network of SVP information services. FIND pioneered the concept of information retailing in the U.S. and now serves the information and research needs of nearly 1,000 organizations. It also publishes and distributes a variety of directories, reference works and information products. In 1974, FIND/SVP's Quick Information Service won the Information Industry Association's Product of the Year Award.

Prior to 1970, Mr. Garvin was Vice President of his own public relations and marketing firm and earlier was a correspondent for *Newsweek*.

A frequent speaker on information-related topics, Mr. Garvin holds a B.A. in political science from Yale University and an M.S. in journalism from the Columbia Graduate School of Journalism. He lives in New York City.

Hubert Bermont did his undergraduate and graduate studies at New York University. For the past twenty-four years he has made his home in Washington, D.C. He is president of Bermont Books, Inc., a consultant and lecturer.

Appendices

Key Sources of Sources

The following is a list of some of the most valuable "sources of sources," directories and guides that list and describe thousands of sources of information. It is by no means all inclusive, but all of the following should be in any good business library.

Business Information Sources
Lorna M. Daniells
University of California Press, 1976

> This is one of the best general source books available. It is a basic, annotated guide to business books and reference sources, bibliographies, indices, abstracts, directories, U.S. and foreign industry statistics, etc. Written by the head of the reference department of Baker Library, Harvard University Graduate School of Business Administration.

Where to Find Business Information
David Brownstone & Gorton Carruth
John Wiley & Sons, 1979

> A useful, handy guide to over 5,000 current sources of information.

Researcher's Guide to Washington
Washington Researchers

> A well written, useful guide to obtaining information from the U.S. Government.

Business Services and Information:
The Guide to the Federal Government
by Management Information Exchange
John Wiley & Sons, 1979

> An all-purpose guide to what's available and where in the Federal Government.

Information Sources
The Membership Directory of the Information Industry Association
316 Pennsylvania Avenue, SE
Washington, DC 20003

> This directory, updated annually, lists 130 information companies and describes their services, publications and data bases.

> The Information Industry Association itself is an excellent source for guidance to available information services.

National Technical Information Services (NTIS)
5285 Port Royal Road
Springfield, VA 22161

> Operated by the U.S. Department of Commerce, NTIS is a source for information on government-sponsored research and other reports prepared by Government agencies. NTIS has a catalogue of available materials and also operates an on-line data base.

Directory Information Service
Gale Research Company
Book Tower
Detroit, MI 48226

> This is a reference periodical covering all types of directories, lists and guides of all kinds. Organized by subject.

Information Market Place
R.R. Bowker Company
1180 Avenue of the Americas
New York, NY 10036

An international directory of information products and services. Lists data bases, information collection centers, retrieval services, publishers, reference books, newsletters, etc.

Directory of Business and Financial Services
Special Libraries Association
235 Park Avenue South
New York, NY 10003

A good guide to key sources.

Monthly Catalog of United States Government Publications
U.S. Government Printing Office
Washington, DC 20402

Arranged alphabetically with an index.

The Encyclopedia of Associations
Gale Research Company
Book Tower
Detroit, MI 48226

The guide to association sources of information.

Consultants and Consulting Organizations Directory
Gale Research Company
Book Tower
Detroit, MI 48226

The best directory of consultants.

Encyclopedia of Information Systems and Services
Gale Research Company
Book Tower
Detroit, MI 48226

An extensive guide to a wide variety of different types of information and research services.

The Directory of Fee-based Information Services
Information Alternative
P.O. Box 657
Woodstock, NY 12498

A paperbound directory listing virtually all known information retrieval services and freelance research firms in the U.S. and Canada.

The Standard Periodical Directory
Oxbridge Communications, Inc.
183 Madison Avenue
New York, NY 10016

Ayer Directory of Publications
Ayer Press
210 W. Washington Square
Philadelphia, PA 19106

Ulrich's International Periodicals Directory
R. R. Bowker Company
1180 Avenue of the Americas
New York, NY 10036

The three leading guides to periodicals. Ulrich's is probably the most extensive, but the other two are quite complete.

International Directory of Marketing Research Houses and Services
New York Chapter, Inc.
American Marketing Association
420 Lexington Avenue
New York, NY 10017

Lists and describes major research firms and services. Published annually.

FINDEX: The Directory of Market Research Reports, Studies and Surveys
FIND/SVP
500 Fifth Avenue
New York, NY 10036

A directory that lists and describes the content of commercially available published research studies.

Directory of Special Libraries and Information Centers
Gale Research Company
Book Tower
Detroit, MI 48226

An extensive, authoritative guide. Includes many small, special libraries in industry.

American Library Directory
R.R. Bowker Company
1180 Avenue of the Americas
New York, NY 10036

The leading guide to public and academic libraries.

Books in Print
R.R. Bowker
1180 Avenue of the Americas
New York, NY 10036

The directory of books. Includes a subject guide to books in print.

Directories of Data Banks

The following is a selected list of major guides to currently available data banks and data-base vendors.

Computer-Readable Data Bases
(A Directory and Data Sourcebook)
American Society for Information Science
1155 Sixteenth St., NW
Washington, DC

> Probably the most complete and definitive directory of computer data bases.

Directory of Online Databases
Cuadra Associates, Inc.
1523 Sixth Street, Suite 12
Santa Monica, CA 90401

> An excellent guide to data bases. Very complete and easy to use.

Directory of On-Line Information Resources
CSG Press
6110 Executive Boulevard, Suite 250
Rockville, MD 20852

> A brief, well-presented listing of data bases.

Computer Bank Book
The Executive Guide to Computer Data Banks
FIND/SVP
500 Fifth Avenue
New York, NY 10036

A layman's guide to computer data banks. Includes examples of computer searches and a selected list of data bases.

Information Retrieval Services

The following is a selected list of some of the leading information retrieval services in the U.S. and Canada. The list is by no means all-inclusive and is restricted to commercial organizations.

Most of the firms listed here offer more than one of the following services: information gathering; custom research; computer data base searching; document retrieval; information consulting.

Bibliographical Center for Research
Rocky Mountain Region, Inc.
245 Columbine, Suite 212
Denver, CO 80206

Capital Systems Group, Inc.
6110 Executive Boulevard
Rockville, MD 20852

Documentation Associates
11720 W. Pico Boulevard
Los Angeles, CA 90064

Editec
53 W Jackson Boulevard
Chicago, IL 60604

FIND/SVP
The Information Clearinghouse
500 Fifth Avenue
New York, NY 10036

FOI Services, Inc.
12315 Wilkins Avenue
Rockville, MD 20852

The Infomart
1 Yonge Street
Toronto, Ontario M5E 1E5 Canada

The Info-Mart
Box 2400
Santa Barbara, CA 93120

Information For Business
25 West 39th Street
New York, NY 10018

Information Management
 Specialists
2010 East 17 Avenue
Denver, CO 80206

Information On Demand
P.O. Box 4536
Berkeley, CA 94704

Arthur D. Little, Inc.
Literature Research Section
25 Acorn Park
Cambridge, MA 02138

National Investment Library
80 Wall Street
New York, NY 10005

Packaged Facts, Inc.
274 Madison Avenue
New York, NY 10016

SVP Canada
Micromedia Ltd
144 Front Street West
Toronto, Ontario M5J 1G2 Canada

Warner-Eddison Associates, Inc.
186 Alewife Brook Parkway
Cambridge, MA 02138

Washington Researchers
910 17th Street, NW
Washington, DC 20006

Washington Service Bureau, Inc.
1225 Connecticut Ave, NW
Washington, DC 20036

World Trade Information Center
1 World Trade Center
New York, NY 10048

World Wide Information
 Services Inc.
600 First Avenue
New York, NY 10016

In addition, a number of academic and public libraries have established divisions that offer computer-data-base searching and/or certain information retrieval services to the public for a fee. Two examples are the "Facts For a Fee" service of the Cleveland Public Library and the "Inform" service of the Minneapolis Public Library.

How-To Books and Guides

The following is a selected list of books that explain how to perform marketing and other forms of research. Some are standard texts; others are more specialized.

Do-it-yourself Marketing Research
George Breen
Mc-Graw-Hill, 1977

Marketing Research
David J. Luck, Hugh G. Wales
 and Donald Taylor, editors
Prentice-Hall, 1974

Industrial Marketing Research
William E. Cox
John Wiley & Sons, 1979

Manual of Industrial Marketing
 Research
Allan Rawnsley, ed.
John Wiley & Sons, 1978

Marketing Research: A Short Course
 for Professionals
Bertram Schoner and Kenneth Uhl
John Wiley & Sons, 1976

Handbook of Marketing Research
Robert Ferber, ed.
McGraw-Hill, 1977

The Modern Researcher
Jacques Barzun and Henry Graff
Harcourt Brace Jovanovich, 1977

Guides to Organiz-ing an Information-Gathering System

If you want to establish a library or information center, here are some helpful sources:

Special Libraries: A Guide for Management (Revised Edition, 1975)
Special Libraries Association
235 Park Avenue South
New York, NY 10003

> This guide describes how to establish a special library. The Association also has other pamphlets, periodicals and services useful to anyone interested in establishing an information center.

American Library Association
50 East Huron Street
Chicago, IL 60611

> This association can also be of assistance in establishing a library.

American Society for Information Science
1010 Sixteenth Street, N.W.
Washington, DC 20036

Another helpful association in the field.

Planning the Special Library
Edited by Ellis Mount
Special Libraries Association (1972)
235 Park Avenue
New York, NY 10003

A Manual of Business Library Practice
Edited by Malcolm J. Campbell
Shoestring Press (1975)
Box 4327, 995 Sherman Avenue
Hamden, CN 06514

A Generalist's Source List

Any librarian or information specialist worth his/her salt will be aghast, but in this appendix we're going to try to give you a brief list of actual sources and services every business generalist should be familiar with, including many of those mentioned in this book.

Those listed here have not been specifically mentioned in the previous appendices, but all are included in one or more of the "Sources of Sources" listed in Appendix I. Thus, we have not listed their addresses here.

Our generalist's source list, then, begins with all the previous appendices. It continues with the following annotated list of items and organizations that should be in any business library, and that every executive should know about.

The *Catalog* of the Bureau of the Census, available from the U.S. Government Printing Office, is a must item because it contains a descriptive list of all the censuses.

The *American Statistics Index*, published by the Congressional Information Service, is a comprehensive guide to the statistical publications of the U.S. Government.

For recent financial statements and other information on publicly-held companies, everyone should have either or both *Moody's Manuals* (Moody's Investors Service) and *Standard & Poors Corporation Records* (standard & Poors).

For general information on various industries there's *Standard & Poors Industry Surveys* and the annual *U.S. Industrial Outlook*, published by the U.S. Department of Commerce.

The *Survey of Buying Power* and *Survey of Industrial Purchasing Power* are two special issues of *Sales and Marketing Management* magazine that should be on every marketing person's shelf.

Basic international data is in the United Nations' *Statistical Yearbook* and *Demographic Yearbook*.

No one can do without Dun & Bradstreet's *Million Dollar Directory* and *Middle Market Directory*, which provide basic information on 70,000 companies with an indicated net worth of $1 million and $0.5 million respectively.

The same applies to Standard & Poor's *Register of Corporations, Directors & Executives*, which includes information on nearly 40,000 companies.

The *Standard Directory of Advertisers* and companion *Directory of Advertising Agencies*, published by the National Register Publishing Company, contain thousands of names of key executives at companies that advertise, as well as their agencies.

The *Thomas' Register of American Manufacturers* and the *Thomas' Register Catalog File* (Thomas Publishing Co.) is a multi-volume set that lists virtually all U.S. manufacturers of any significance, alphabetically and by product, and also contains reproduced product catalogs.

The Dun & Bradstreet *Reference Book* is probably the most complete published list of companies and includes their principal SIC number and estimated financial-strength rating. It is available only to customers of Dun & Bradstreet's Business Information Reports.

Business Publication Rates and Data, published by the Standard Rate & Data Service, contains a wealth of information on all business publications. Standard Rate & Data also publishes similar directories covering consumer publications, other media and direct mail lists. The entire set should be in every library.

Who's Who In America is published by Marquis Who's Who which also has companion directories.

Sources of State Information & State Industrial Directories, available from the Chamber of Commerce of the United States, is a key to locating regional information.

The *Statistical Abstract of the United States*, published by the U.S. Bureau of the Census, is an information "bible" that includes a wealth of industrial, social, political and economic statistics.

So is the *Information Please Almanac*, published annually by Simon & Schuster.

No one should forget two reference basics: The New *Encyclopedia Britannica* and Webster's *Third New International Dictionary of the English Language*.

The published index to articles in business periodicals is *Business Periodicals Index*, published by H.W. Wilson.

The published index to articles in general and non-technical publications is the *Reader's Guide to Periodical Literature*, also published by H.W. Wilson.

And *the* index to current information on companies and industries is the *F & S Index of Corporations & Industries*, produced by Predicasts, Inc. In fact, Predicasts has so many other important information services and products that its brochures should be in your files immediately.

Statistics Sources (Gale Research Company) is a good subject guide to data on industrial, business, social, educational, financial and other topics.

National Directory of Newsletters and Reporting Services (Gale Research Company). Offers a list of newsletters in all fields.

While you're at it, get a list of all the publications of the Gale Research Company.

In case it isn't obvious, every business should subscribe to *Business Week, Forbes* and the *Harvard Business Review* as well as *The New York Times* and *The Wall Street Journal*. Beyond that, your own activities will determine which periodicals you should get. *Management Contents* is a handy bi-weekly periodical (published by Management Contents, Inc.) that reprints the tables of contents of some 300 leading business journals. The quarterly *Information Catalog* (published by FIND/SVP) keeps you updated on new studies and reference tools in a variety of different industries.

(We have not included basic business textbooks, almanacs and dictionaries, because these are easily accessible in any public library. Also, they are listed in Lorna Daniells' book *Business Information Sources*, which we referred to in the introduction.)

All businesses should be familiar with the activities of The Conference Board, the American Management Association and the Research Institute of America (all in New York City). They publish a wide variety of information products, services and studies collectively useful to virtually everyone.

Finally, here's a list of other key information companies of wide interest (with a very brief outline of their activities), some of whose products or services should probably be readily accessible to you. Find out more about them.

A.C. Nielsen Company Northbrook, IL	Provides marketing and media research services; also petroleum information services.
Arthur D. Little Cambridge, MS	A leading research and consulting firm.
Aspen Systems Corporation Germantown, MD	Information and litigation management services and publications in the healthcare field.
Auerbach Publishers, Inc. Pennsauken, NJ	Data processing and computer information.
Battelle Memorial Institute Columbus, OH	Another important research firm.
The Bureau of National Affairs Washington, DC	Major publisher of looseleaf reporting services for business and professional use.
Business International Corporation New York, NY	Research and information on foreign countries, companies and industries.
Chase Econometric Associates Bala Cynwyd, PA	Economic analysis, forecasting and consulting.
Congressional Information Service Washington, DC	A leading indexer and micropublisher of government documents.

Data Courier, Inc. Louisville, KY	Publisher of abstracts and indexes in scientific and business management areas.
Data Resources, Inc. Lexington, MS	Issues forecasts based on computerized econometric models.
Disclosure, Inc. Washington, DC	The primary source for reports filed with the Securities & Exchange Commission.
Dun & Bradstreet, Inc. New York, NY	Provides a very wide variety of information services mostly on companies and industries.
Economic Information Services New York, NY	Provides information on companies and industrial plants.
Environment Information Center New York, NY	A clearinghouse for energy and environmental information.
FIND/SVP New York, NY	The leading information retrieval service.
Frost & Sullivan, Inc. New York, NY	A large publisher of industry studies.
Information Handling Services Englewood, CO	A leading supplier of technical data such as manufacturers' catalogs and industrial standards and codes.
Institute for Scientific Information Philadelphia, PA	Provides a complete line of services for people in the sciences.
International Data Corporation Waltham, MS	Provides information on the computer industry.

McGraw-Hill New York, NY	A leading publisher and information service company in many areas; especially construction and real estate. Parent company of Standard & Poor.
R.R. Bowker Company New York, NY	A leading publisher of reference directories.
Stanford Research Institute Menlo Park, CA	Similar to Battelle with special strength in chemicals.
Time, Inc. New York, NY	A leading publisher; owner of S.A.M.I., a syndicated marketing information service.
TRW Business Credit Services Orange, CA	Provides credit information on business locations.

Excluded from the above list are individual data bases and data base vendors covered in a previous Appendix, as well as other sources previously mentioned.

INDEX

A

B

I

K

L

M

N

O

S

T

U

V

W

Xerox, 25

This book has been set in 11 point Univers light with 60 point Avant Garde, extra light display chapter heads—7 points leaded. Typesetting was prepared by Alert Arts, Springfield, VA.